Collected Poems of Bronwen Wallace

Collected Poems of
Bronwen Wallace

Edited by Carolyn Smart

McGill-Queen's University Press
Montreal & Kingston • London • Chicago

ISBN 978-0-2280-0187-4 (cloth)
ISBN 978-0-2280-0321-2 (ePDF)
ISBN 978-0-2280-0322-9 (ePUB)

Legal deposit second quarter 2020
Bibliothèque nationale du Québec

Printed in Canada on acid-free paper that is 100% ancient forest free (100% post-consumer recycled), processed chlorine free

Funded by the Government of Canada | Financé par le gouvernement du Canada | Canada | Canada Council for the Arts | Conseil des arts du Canada

We acknowledge the support of the Canada Council for the Arts.

Nous remercions le Conseil des arts du Canada de son soutien.

Library and Archives Canada Cataloguing in Publication

Title: Collected poems of Bronwen Wallace / edited by Carolyn Smart.
Other titles: Poems
Names: Wallace, Bronwen, author. | Smart, Carolyn, 1952- editor.
Identifiers: Canadiana (print) 20200169165 | Canadiana (ebook) 20200169173 | ISBN 9780228001874 (hardcover) | ISBN 9780228003212 (PDF) | ISBN 9780228003229 (EPUB)
Subjects: LCGFT: Poetry.
Classification: LCC PS8595 .A56504 2020 | DDC C811/.54—dc23

Contents

Signs of the Former Tenant

Moving Away from the Past

Between Words

Introduction

This started out as a simple poem
for Virginia Woolf
it wasn't going to mention history
or choices or women's lives
the complexities of women's friendships
or the countless gritty details
of an ordinary woman's life
that never appear in poems at all

yet even as I write these words
those ordinary details intervene
between the poem I meant to write
and this one   where the delicate faces
of my children   faces of friends
of women I have never even seen
glow on the blank pages
and deeper than any silence
press around me
waiting their turn

"A Simple Poem for Virginia Woolf"

To read a Bronwen Wallace poem is to enter a conversation, a nonlinear dialogue that explores history, personal stories, grief, tenderness, and the intricate details of everyday life. As Dennis Lee described her style in his obituary for Bronwen published in the *Globe and Mail* on 26 August 1989: "It's a loopy, lopey canter through domestic vignettes, childhood memories, snatches of yarning and yack with women friends, plus alternate takes and digressions all hopscotching through lives and generations linked in a rich random tapestry, maybe punctuated by notions picked up from neurology or pre-history, with the whole lit up by passages of luminous musings on the workaday mystery of being human."

Bronwen, the healthiest person most of us knew, died at the age of forty-four, after a skyrocketing literary career of nine years that included four collections of poetry. After her death a collection of essays, a volume of short stories, and a final collection of poems were published. To read the poems today is as intimate an experience as it was during her lifetime. Her voice is as clear and timely as it was then, her narrative gift a form of support and guidance for friends and casual readers alike. It was a style she developed over the years, entirely her own, that Dennis Lee termed "female narrative form." Reading the poems is like sitting down to a long and necessary talk with a close friend.

To be her friend was to be included in what felt both intensely intimate and communal. You couldn't walk down the street with her without encountering several people who would update her on their lives: the woman running for city council; the woman she'd counselled and consoled through difficult times; the founder of a newly organized men's sharing group; the students she'd taught at Queen's or at St Lawrence College. She was a confidante and mentor to a host of people from diverse spheres. When she was dying, there was a wicker basket next to her bed filled to overflowing with cards and letters from people most of her caregiving group had never heard of: the widespread network who had been touched by her and involved in the many aspects of her life. More than seven hundred people attended her funeral.

We met for the first time in 1981 at a reading she hosted in Kingston. I had driven one of the readers from Toronto where I was then living, because I wanted to meet her: she'd published several of my earliest poems in *Quarry* magazine, which she edited from 1978 through 1981. Her mentorship of emerging writers, and especially women writers, stemmed from those years, first as the assistant to the poet Gail Fox and then as editor of the magazine. The poet and professor Kateri Lanthier remembers that Bronwen warmly encouraged her early poems, accepting two for issue 24/4 of *Quarry* when Kateri was sixteen years old. The author Helen Humphreys was one of the winners of a high school writing competition in *Quarry* magazine in the late 1970s, judged by Bronwen. She states: "It was my first ever publication, and went a long way to giving me the confidence to continue along the poetry path."

From our first meeting onwards, she was a source of joy and fun: she would invite me to stay with her for the weekend and we'd paint our faces in Day-Glo and walk around City Park eating gelato cones; we'd go on the Kingston Trolley Tour and she'd offer a hilarious, loud revisionist history in contrast to the bland official overvoice. She was a poet starting to publish at the same time as I was: we'd practise reading our poems together and several times had joint public readings. I recall how nervous she was to read the poem that appears (in part) at the beginning of this essay as she feared a backlash against its feminist stance. The year she read at the annual general meeting of the League of Canadian Poets was the year the Feminist Caucus was formed and announced. One member of the league shouted out: "If there's going to be a feminist caucus, then there should be a Nazi caucus," so her fears were not unfounded.

She was also politically unrelenting. When I mentioned I was voting in the upcoming federal election she reproved me with "Why vote? It just encourages them." When I told her I was to marry the man she'd introduced me to mere weeks earlier, she didn't chastise me for my haste, but for the fact that I allowed the state any involvement in my personal life. She was fierce in response to class and gender bias; she was supportive of vulnerability like no one else I knew. She was challenging and loving, in equal measure. Her ability to analyze a situation and – crucially – to offer a constructive suggestion for progression was unparalleled. To say that I miss her in these confusing days is the ultimate understatement.

For those who knew her well, rereading her work today feels uplifting and consoling. The poems will welcome those who didn't know her to a voice that speaks to any decade: a voice filled with empathy, anger, love, and a passion for social justice; a voice that speaks from experience and with warmth. To read the poems as they are collected here is to trace the journey of a writer discovering her own strengths. From the earliest poems, where she fleshed out experience through colloquial language and syntax, through the final poems that read like the music they admire and echo, the reader is caught up in a verbal relationship, a friendship with language and the woman who created it. "Welcome," she says, and somehow it feels she is welcoming you into your own life.

This collection could be named "Blueprints for a Larger Life," an indication of what the reader may garner from these generous-hearted poems. That title was, in fact, the one she used for the keynote address she offered at her final public appearance, on International Women's Day 1989, in Kingston, Ontario, only days after she'd been diagnosed with the cancer of the mouth that swiftly took her life. But to start at the beginning, as she rarely did in her poems – they'd loop all around personal history, with the magic of stories told and retold – Bronwen was born in Kingston, Ontario, on 26 May 1945. Her mother, Marguerite (Peggy), was a teacher, and her father, Ferdinand, a metal worker at Alcan. Her only sibling, Cameron, was born in December 1949. Bronwen's formal education took place entirely in Kingston where she completed her BA and MA in English language and literature at Queen's University, writing a master's thesis in 1968 on Lewis Carroll's *Alice in Wonderland*, titled "A Choice of Madness: A Study of Alice's Adventures as Myth, Reflecting the Victorian Dilemma."

Her doctoral studies were interrupted by student activism, and finally abandoned, as she developed deep political beliefs on the Queen's University campus, as many did on campuses across the world in the 1960s and '70s. She was drawn to Marxism and subsequently to what was then known as the women's movement. She joined a group of feminists who chained themselves to the parliamentary gallery in the House of Commons as part of a two-day demonstration for abortion rights in May 1970, and from there she offered a pro-choice speech. Realizing that she spent more time involved in politics than in academia, she left Kingston to travel across Canada, eventually settling in Windsor, Ontario, with her partner Ron Baxter and becoming active in a women's co-op bookstore, union organizing, and finding shelter and new identities for those fleeing the Vietnam War draft. When their son Jeremy was born in 1974, Bronwen helped start a co-op daycare.

Meantime, she admired the political and work-focused poetry of writers such as Philip Levine and the stories of Alice Munro, recognizing that she too honoured landscape and the language of ordinary people. Opening Al Purdy's poetry collection *The Cariboo Horses*, she cried with relief to discover someone who understood that lilacs flower in May in most of Canada as opposed to everything she'd been taught in school about the English Romantic tradition, and that the rocky Shield country of Eastern Ontario where she had always felt most at home was a terrain that also nurtured poetry. She moved back to Kingston then, and she never left.

Her political involvements beginning in the mid-1960s, and particularly her profound connection to feminism, led her to think about women's conversations in different ways. As she said in a talk given as part of a panel on women and language for the Feminist Caucus of the League of Canadian Poets AGM in 1987: "I begin with what I have been given: women's stories, women's conversations. Since most of these stories come to me in pretty straightforward, conversational language, that's what I use in the poem. But as I begin to recreate that conversation on the page, I begin to listen to the voice that tells these stories, a voice that is angry sometimes, or frightened, or grieving or ecstatic. And it becomes the voice I have heard in so many women's conversations, a voice that explores *both* the events in the story itself, *and* something else that lies within those events … What I hear in 'ordinary conversation' is that movement that goes on among us when we feel safe enough or confident enough or loved enough to explore the power within us."

That voice grew through her early work (some of which is collected at the end of this volume) and eventually became her first collection of poetry, published in 1980 jointly with the poems of Mary di Michele in a volume entitled *Bread and Chocolate / Marrying into the Family*. Geographically and emotionally, Bronwen centred herself directly within the landscape where both her mother's and father's families had lived for more than 150 years, land she knew "*like the back of my hand*, we say / for the place we come to call home" ("Distance from Harrowsmith to Tamworth"). That history, of both blood family and chosen family, was the source material for her work for the rest of her life. She mixed it with her usual ingredients – labour, feminism, and location (the politics of place) – for she knew better than most that poetry is large and able to accommodate everything.

Her craft broadened through the second and third volumes: *Signs of the Former Tenant* (1983), which won the Pat Lowther Award, and especially *Common Magic* (1985) reveal her increasing sense of the possibilities of narrative, the many conversations and points of view that can be accommodated within an openhearted, digressive style. Reviewers found in *Signs* "a new capaciousness of poetic personality and a residual sense of the beauty of life (symbolized quite often as streams of light in domestic settings) which steps past the impediments of feminist writing, and is refreshing after the complacency, almost bigotry of much recipe writing about womanhood" (Terry Whalen, *Canadian Literature* 103). *Common Magic* garnered similar commentary: "A number of convenient labels come to mind: feminist, political, introspective, sensitive, homely ... Wallace's narrator emerges as the inventor-historian, always interpreting and re-interpreting these imposed 'stories in a foreign language'" (Gary Boire, *Canadian Literature* 110). Only four years later, in an obituary which begins "A wonderful poet is gone," Dennis Lee was to write that "much of her energy went into creating a new poetic instrument: 'female narrative form,' and learning to play it." The zeitgeist had shifted.

Her life and work were deeply marked by two events: the death of her close friend Pat Logan ("The Cancer Poems") and her work as a counsellor in the mid-1980s for Kingston Interval House, a shelter for battered women and their children ("Bones").

Throughout her poetry there is the strong belief that everyday things are magical, and her fourth collection, *The Stubborn Particulars of Grace* (1987), reveals this awareness most directly. The title highlights consistent themes throughout her work: the frequent use of the word *stubborn*, luminescent details of the particular, and the sense of the spiritual within all things, as she writes in "Particulars," the poem that closes the collection:

> And to say for myself, just once,
> without embarrassment, *bless*,
> thrown out as to some lightness
> that I actually believe in,
> surprised (as I believe
> they were) to find it
> here, where it seems impossible
> that one life even matters, though
> like them, I'll argue
> the stubborn argument of the particular,
> right now, in the midst of things, *this*
> and *this*.

What changed as her poetry progressed was her ability to encompass more, to let the poems go their own way and find their own rhythm outside the narrative. Different voices in the poems speak in different cadences; competing or parallel narratives appear within single poems. Within this collection you will also see her increased use of epigraphs and quotations from other authors: a direct attempt to introduce as many other voices as possible into the literary conversation that she continued to create.

She'd tell people that it was characters speaking directly to her that led to the short fiction she wrote in the posthumously published volume *People You'd Trust Your Life To* (1990), but she never abandoned poetry. "One of the things that makes my poetry strong is a very recognizable voice. In the stories (*People You'd Trust Your Life To*) I try to expand that voice. It's a first collection and has its weaknesses but it taught me some interesting things about voice that I'm now able to apply to the new poems," she told Janice Williamson early in 1989. At the end of her life she was writing poems inspired by the work of country-music singer Emmylou Harris and wild narratives based on "scientific facts" from the tabloids (as in the poem "Miracles" where the epigraphs relate stories of weeping Elvis paintings, or pictures of Jesus on a freezer), which comprise the second section of the posthumous collection *Keep That Candle Burning Bright and Other Poems* (1991). Within this volume she challenges artistic and class assumptions through both content and voice, a voice confident enough to assume that the raw honesty and testimony of country music can be a further component of our humanity.

This collection gathers all the poems she published in book form, offered chronologically to reveal the growth of her expansive confidence, and ends with a selection of unpublished work, all of it written before 1983. In these earlier pieces the reader will recognize what became her poetic obsessions: family, work, relationships, the details of ordinary life.

A committee of nineteen Kingston-area writers, activists, academics, and friends met for more than two years to put together the 2008 conference Common Magic: The Legacy of Bronwen Wallace, which took place over a few days marked by a particularly powerful snowstorm. Award-winning poets, journalists, activists, academics, visual artists, musicians, family, and friends came together in Kingston to honour and reflect upon Bronwen Wallace's legacy. What began as an idea for a gathering of a small group of people in one room blossomed into a three-day event that examined Bronwen's influence on Canadian literature, feminist activism, and local journalism. The events included over fifty presenters spanning three generations of writers who spoke about the influence of Bronwen upon their work (her poetry, her ability to address memory, the impact of domestic violence in her work, her correspondence with other award-winning women writers); screenings of two films by Bronwen Wallace and her life partner Chris Whynot; a theatre performance influenced by Bronwen's words performed by Queen's University drama students; a world premiere of a choral piece inspired by Bronwen's work called *Requiem,* composed by Jennifer Bennett and performed by Queen's Polyhymnia Choir; an opening of a visual art display by Queen's art students in response to Bronwen's words; one of the last concerts given by Kate and Anna McGarrigle to a crowd of more than five hundred; and reflections by Bronwen's family members.

Today, younger poets such as Sarah Yi-Mei Tsiang and Kim Fahner openly acknowledge her influence. Julie Berry remembered Bronwen in the Brick Books online weekly series on literary influences: "When asked the after-reading question, 'Is there a poet who inspired you?' my answer is Walt Whitman. He set my hair on fire. But it was Bronwen Wallace who gave me permission to write in my own voice. I also like to share the piece of advice I took from one of her interviews or essays – words she attributed to Diane Arbus: 'The more specific you are, the more general it'll be.' A writer can live and work and breathe by those words." Since 1994, the Writers' Trust of Canada (in recent years, with the financial support of the Royal Bank of Canada) has sponsored a major prize named the Bronwen Wallace Award for Emerging Writers. That award has celebrated – and introduced to the reading public – the work of writers such as Stephanie Bolster, Rachel Rose, Alissa York, Sonnet L'Abbé, Michael Crummey, Noor Naga, John Elizabeth Stintzi, Alison Pick, Brendan Bowles, and Alessandra Naccarato, amongst others.

Her work continues to resonate today. In April 2019, her friend and fellow poet Erin Mouré wrote:

> Bronwen's poetry was not just about the urgency of descriptive image, the narrative and its final punch, the voice-over narration; it was also and ever the line-end, the rhythm, the torque of that rhythm. The assemblage, that made the poem whole, made her readers whole. She would take a narrational surface and show how each detail of its depth, and each nuance in us as readers – that we feel as personal confusion and doubt – is present in the surface of the poem and in fact constructs it, a surface deceptive in its smooth realism. Her work in the poem was one of those first musical backbeats of 1970s and '80s Canadian feminism, of the struggle for civil rights for women, heard everywhere, radical and open. Her poems still have their recombinatory power.

Bronwen was a challenging, loving, wise, and tireless friend. We miss all that her work might have offered us: the clarity, tenderness, righteous anger, and inclusivity of her voice. Thirty years on, we have her vibrant poems in print once again. I hope new readers will be drawn to these poems as she had hoped people would be, "like guide posts to a mystery at the center of any story," as she said to Janice Williamson. We need her fierce insight more than ever.

CAROLYN SMART
Harrowsmith, 2019

Marrying into the Family

MARRIAGES

After the wedding in the parlour
where her sisters were married
and her father's sisters before them
she comes with her new husband
to his family farm
to the kitchen with its woodstove
where his mother cooked
to the polished table in the dining-room
and the cupboard where she stores
her mother's crystal
her grandmother's china

she will put the quilt
her aunt made on the bed upstairs
where her husband was born
where she will give birth
and one day her daughter will take
her china and her linens
to the beds and tables
of women she is not related to
except by marriage
except by the using of the things
they used

the men move in their own lines
fences and ploughed fields the same farm
all of their lives father to son
but what the women own
they carry with them
and in their husbands' homes
perform this marriage
of things touched and shared
woman to woman

back and forth across a county
they weave beyond blood lines
the stubborn pattern
of their own
particular ceremonies

OLD PHOTOGRAPHS

I'm told the effect is merely technical
something to do with shutter speeds
and the size of the lens
the way the children seem starched
like the dresses they wear for the occasion
the adults behind them rigid and unsmiling
in their dark suits and heavy dresses

but that does not explain the eyes
how the calm there is repeated
in the sure tilt of a chin
in the way hands lie
loosely folded in the lap
until each figure emerges
as if carved from the furniture
and rounded by the room
where these photographs take place
where each family gathered
for the marriage of its daughters
where Christmas was held
the dead laid out
where family portraits
line the walls and cluster on little tables
each generation stiffening
for the obligatory photograph

was it the slow closing of the shutter
that held them
staring beyond the camera
did they notice its blink
or was it the room itself
that pressed into their limbs
gathered itself
behind the calm and open eyes

GREAT AUNT

Everyone says she's remarkable
for 93   her mind so clear
most of the time which just proves
that hard work never killed anyone
and she did work hard
Uncle Bill can remember her
doing up tomatoes   more jars
than he could count as a boy
in the summer she'd be right up there
pitching hay along with the men
and the bread she baked at threshing time
twenty loaves easy in a morning
though she can't for the life of her
remember the recipe now
and Aunt June says well mother
it doesn't matter
and I suppose it doesn't
but I can't take my eyes off
her hands kneading the soft air
punching and rolling
the smooth shapes of her memories
rising with the smell of the yeast
till her arms are
lean and brown again
lifting the brown loaves from the oven
lifting the brown hay up
to the wagon and the sun
strong behind her

CONNECTING

It gets handed down
along with the china fruit bowl
and it's a good story about
my great-grandmother
getting so angry with
her husband's drinking that
she went right into the bar
one evening and ordered drinks
on the house   my great-grandfather
so embarrassed he never went back
this being 1895 or so when
respectable women never went
to bars

That's about it.
Not enough for a poem really
even with the fruit bowl
which is delicate and well-made
but both of them just kind of
sit there   refuse to relinquish
the appropriate metaphors

And my mother can't give me
much else   only remembers
sitting with her in the evenings
her parents out somewhere
and the old woman's hands too shaky
to light a lamp   so my mother
would stick kindling in the stove
wave it flaring in the room
like a torch
her grandmother never saying a word
never warning her about fire

Something begins to emerge then
the shape of the old woman
the little flares of light falling
to a glow around her
the kitchen suddenly quiet as
the bar became when she entered
the triumphant flicker of a smile
beside her husband's silence
on the dark walk home
Not much to build a poem on
shapes so delicate
like the china bowl filled with fruit
glowing in the centre
of my kitchen table

THE FAMILY SAINTS AND THE DINING-ROOM TABLE

Everyone remembers how beautiful they were
the ones who spent most of their adult life
dying of consumption
and how lovely the others looked
laid out with their dead babies beside them
They love to tell about the great-aunt
who died of strep-throat on her honeymoon
although there are no photographs to show her
smiling beside her intended husband
and the only thing anyone remembers
about the second cousin with the goiter
is that when the country doctor tried to remove it
he sliced the jugular vein instead

But no-one talks at all
about great-grandmother who refused
to go to hospital for the tumour
and had two doctors come in
to remove it while she lay chloroformed
on her own dining-room table
(after which she went on living
for another twenty years)
though they remember how her son's wife
wouldn't have the table in the house
said it made her sick to eat off it
so they gave it to the aunt
who was an old maid
and she kept it
which everyone said just proved
how queer she was for why
any decent woman would want
a thing like that in the house
they couldn't understand

THE MAIDEN AUNTS

They are the ones who in Victorian novels
fade into the pages
with a discreet hint of lavender
and though the modern style is robust well-tailored
though voices are shrill and they hold
important positions in offices hospitals
something about them requires still
a certain delicacy
shadowy tales of jiltings   grand renunciations
in the name of religion or family loyalty

And they are loyal   at family occasions
they arrange themselves on the edges of snapshots
like the sprays of green around
the florist roses   the anniversary couple
or the newly christened nephew
they are small talk
for the other relatives   anecdotes
slipped by-the-by between
good marriages and the family resemblance
of a second cousin

The maiden aunts have no
claim to their father
though they retain his name
it issues sideways from their mouths
lacking their brothers' style
sprawled like the family farms
across the county map
while their mother claims
the married sisters
who wear her wifely postures
as they settle into middle age
clustered by growing children
and although the maiden aunts inherit

the peculiar shape of an ancestral nose
or the exact shading of their grandmother's eyes
something in their faces
makes these features seem
incongruous like the photograph
that catches its subject unaware
startles into being
an attitude so unexpected
that the most familiar relative stares for a moment
before she tosses the thing aside   turns
impatiently to poses more appropriate
for gilt-edged albums
but in the corner of some unused drawer
these other photographs
keep their surprised expressions
released from family obligations
their unguarded gestures
seem to open to the dark
like renegade flowers

FINDING MY REAL ANCESTORS

I can only trace
the family tree
through two generations
before stepmothers
insinuate themselves
like characters
from the Brothers Grimm
blocking my way
to the real ancestors
whom no-one now remembers

not that it's uncommon
I've seen family plots
in old church cemeteries
one big patriarchal stone
surrounded by smaller female ones
the dates of their deaths
a neat progression
across his longer span

even in my grandmother's stories
her stepmother's arrival
when she was three was
just another detail
like her first party dress
or her wedding
stories I half heard
or later asked for simply
to humour her

and her diary's mostly dates
the births of her children
weddings   funerals
then on a separate page for
April 1920 (she'd be
35 or so)
her one memory
of her real mother

lies in my hand
like the key to an old trunk
scraping against the lock
lid thrown back
the questions
I never thought to ask
spilling into the room

DARK FIELDS

In the photographs my grandmother
is heavy in her straight chair
her skirts stiffening the crippled leg
which I never see although
it is always there
after the incident with the horse
who never appears at all
is legendary
like my grandmother's skill with him
or the promised horses of my childhood
but I keep holding the negatives
at different angles to the light
squinting my eyes
for a glimpse of our white figures
galloping toward each other
over the dark fields

HEREDITY

After the incident
my mother reassures me
it's a simple operation
really   your knee
should be as good as new
in six weeks or so

On the way to the OR
I remember only
my mother's stories
my grandmother
thrown from a buggy
kneecap smashed
the crutch she used
for the rest of her life

Now I lie
on this stiff bed
and think I feel
the bones
of a woman I never knew
knit themselves
under my familiar skin

GRANDMA WAGAR'S DOUBLE BIND

In those days of course
a woman stayed home
until she married
and my grandmother
used to say
she had nothing to show
for her ten years of teaching
because she gave all her salary
to her father

The man she married
(against her father's wishes)
was a good husband but
a poor farmer
when times got bad
he put a mortgage on the farm
by forging her signature
in 1927 they lost
everything

Then she took in mending
because in those days of course
a woman stayed home
after she'd married

BEHIND THE PHOTOGRAPH

There's this photo of my grandmother at 25
in an elaborate hat of creamy satin
with a great dark feather that lifts
almost as proudly as the profile beneath it
the tilted chin and sweep of rich black hair
all that I know of this woman
her famous skill with horses
her grace as a dancer   distills here
in what could be
the cover for a novel
where despite her father's objections
and the young man's poverty
the heroine marries
the one she loves

Not far from the truth
given my grandfather
who began their marriage spending
all the wedding money on an opal ring
which she wore all her life
though year after year
he wanted to pawn it
for the schemes that sprang
like weeds from the dust of his farm
and when they lost the land
he said it was her fault
scorned her for begging
credit from the grocer and
taking in mending

something in her he hated even then
a stubbornness perhaps that took directions
he hadn't expected   the way later
he hated the disease
that crippled her

till in the final years he'd
take away her crutch
leave her weighted
to the chair   the fat old woman
of the last photographs
defeated   eyes turned
from the man beside her

When I was six
my father took me to a beach
where beneath the dunes
he told me a hotel was buried
and all day I spent
digging   expectant that any moment
my shovel would strike stone
sun flash on the scarlet tip
of a shingle   just as now
lights of green and amber
glow like secrets in the opal
my grandmother left
well-kept promises that keep me
sifting the stories
the photographs for something
I'm supposed to find
the movement just before
the shutter click
lift of a chin that
even beneath the rolls of fat
brings the bones of a young woman
into profile   or the defiant
moving of a crutch behind a chair
in every photograph its absence
a statement like the straight set
of the shoulders   the almost careless way
the hands are folded
gestures that move
out from behind the photograph

to frame it in another way
like the gestures I leave out
in my memory of wet sand
tears and my father calling me home
the way my hand clenched
around the handle of a shovel
and the arm's arc again
and again into sand
my back turned
from the waves
and the sun's inviting dance

THE KINGDOM OF THE FATHERS

In the lands I used to visit
my grandfather reigned larger
than the giants of my nursery books
and the names of the villages along the highway
were merely signposts to his kingdom
where the half-heard tales of his exploits
how he carried children out
from burning farmhouses
or saved a crop in a hard summer
spread in my imagination
like the stains on his kitchen wall
marks of his rage
unsatisfactory pots of tea   whole plates of meat
thrown over the heads of wife and family

In those days I believed that all kings
smelled of peppermint and pipe tobacco
and sat in great chairs whose covers
chafed my knees as I climbed up
through the great claps of laughter
to his face   even after he died
his eyes burned through the dark
to my dreams   more real
than the wife he left
the stick-figure grandmother
with her frail stories and
nervous hands
like the grey sampler on the wall
ABCs in careful script
and the tight-lipped message
  Idleness is the parent
  of vice and misery
    7 August, 1894
so neat in its heavy frame
it hinders the easy arithmetic

addition from birthdate to the fact
that she was nine then
my grandfather twenty
already owned a farm
a household of women
mother and sisters hovering
around him
and while he set himself
against drought and rain
my grandmother sat
in the stiff heat of the afternoon
and stitched

Did she dream of princes then
and ten years later
maybe his notice of her
the pride in her father's smile
and the envious eyes of friends
carried magic enough
for the next 50 years
perhaps
but I don't know what shapes
his death took in her dreams
or whether a day came
when stepping into the kitchen
she saw how the stains he'd left
flattened into the wall
and his chair sat
ordinary in the corner
or how the grey script
of her sampler
curled like ivy
in its frame

PROFILE

The living swim through their photographs
like fish
even the ones taken yesterday
cannot contain them
and it does not matter
which we choose
for the family album where
through the flicker of a page
the scrawny six-year-old can twist
and turn herself to bride or mother

But the dead move differently
though they seem fixed forever
on uncomfortable chairs
or grimly posed beside ageing husbands
and though we search nervously
through overflowing boxes desperate
for happier expressions more
august occasions the dead
retreat behind their frozen attitudes
and the yellowing surfaces cloud
with their wishes
their unfinished business
till we become like the man
who sorts through photographs
of someone he once loved
and is held not by the ones
that catch her full-faced to the camera
but the tentative profile
where the pattern
of shadows on her face and the way
her hair falls through them
imply a movement so hesitant

he cannot remember
which way she turned
when the shutter
reopened

MARRYING INTO THE FAMILY

In the early snapshots
flanked by his beautiful sisters
she smiles apologetically
for small breasts
thin hair
Even the wedding portrait
is diffident
although her gown is quite becoming
(his mother wore a mink)

When the children came
she denied any resemblance
For years they believed they had
only one grandfather
and were not present
at her father's funeral

Christmases they spent
with his people
the children of course included
in the family photograph
She held the camera
(until his brother married   then
she stood to the side
encouraged the children
to smile)

When her knees stiffened with arthritis
her doctor advised a cane
she goes without one
in deference to his eldest sister
a retired gym teacher
who at 69
still jogs two miles a day

On their fiftieth anniversary
the children financed
a professional portrait
she wears the mink stole
his mother left her
the photograph is lovely although
her eyes are slightly puffy
(she always was
allergic to fur)

RITES

My mother was a teacher
every morning running
for the bus
the other mothers
slippered and pincurled
watching from their kitchens

I called for Barb on my way to school
Barb's mother in a pink housecoat
sipped coffee inspected me
for flaws *your mother*
should take care of you
pulling my hat down
hard over my ears

So I learned to pretend
a mother fat and pink
and pincurled in a huge kitchen
surrounded by coffee cups

But at night
when they spoke
in my mother's kitchen
of indifferent husbands
pregnant daughters
I imagined her
like the witches in my books
passing in the market place
the village women signing
against the evil eye
but coming by dark
to her cottage
the young girls seeking
love potions
the married women
ergot .

STRIPPING FURNITURE

The family says
that Grandma painted the rocker
for each new baby

And after two days
of scraping at stubborn layers
of thick white paint
I can believe it   begin to think
I must be crazy   cooped up
in this stuffy room
the smell of the thinner
making me sick
knowing the kid won't recognize
the difference between this rocker
and one I could buy
second-hand somewhere

And why would *she* bother?
When would she have the time
what with milking and canning
and meals for the threshers and
a half-dozen other kids
the grandmother I remember
as brittle as this paint and
so stubborn you'd think
she'd have a kid
in the barn somewhere
and go right back to the milking
isn't that how it is anyway
after seven or eight?

I reach for the scraper
slide back another layer
pushing toward
some afternoon in late summer
supper warming on the stove
kids playing on the porch   a baby
crying in the back bedroom
and the woman I begin to imagine
with hair the colour of soft bare wood
squatting heavily beside this rocking-chair
dipping her brush

GETTING DOWN TO IT

The yellowing photographs again
aunts cousins grandmothers
spread out on the table
while I search their faces
for clues messages
find only my own face anticipated
in the shape of a nose
the process of my own ageing
traced in the lines around mouth and eyes

their photographs remain silent
the framed blank faces staring into space
are not their gifts
they did not choose these postures
these angles of sunlight
did not even imagine me here
waiting behind the photographer

what they left was
more accidental   things tossed up
from the daily clutter
pieces of china   silverware
the odd bit of embroidery
a recipe for plum jam
things they may have planned
to hand on   perhaps even
told stories to go with them
some little incident
to decorate the thing
and things their hands touched
without ever thinking of stories
or even of the need for them
the stories themselves gone now anyway
each repetition shaping them
to other people's memories

so that only the things remain
arbitrary like the dates
of birth marriage death
scrawled in the family bible
carved on tombstones
without story or memory
to round them out
flat as the blank faces
the arranged poses
as silent as the bones
I can't see in the photographs

though they remain somewhere and
this cup a great-grandmother used
the jars of plum jam in my cellar
remain
all I have
to go by

COUNTRY AUCTION SALE

Nearest the auctioneer a small group
of men from the district – farmers mostly –
are bidding on a chain-saw, grease-guns
rolls of chicken wire, oil cans
baskets of odd tools
cans of nails

Behind them young couples
the women in long dresses
the men in embroidered shirts and patched jeans
are waiting for a cane rocker or
a loveseat, china soup tureens
pickle crocks, old milk cans

Later the crowd will move out
to the waiting cars and trucks
the farmers returning to their chores
to the farms they hold from their fathers
and the young couples
will drive back to the city
carrying their treasures
the unknown ghosts
they have bought
to inhabit their households

ON A COUNTRY ROAD

Ahead of me
my son triumphant
on his father's shoulders
rides full-gallop over slippery gravel
my cries
at unexpected pot-holes
low-hanging branches
muted in his laughter

A camera clicks us
into place

the undeveloped snapshot
slipping from the black box
transforms our gestures
and ten seconds later
we emerge
attitudes on 3 x 3
In the foreground
slightly blurred
a small boy smiling
atop a man's slim shoulders
behind them
the figure of a woman
face shaded
by the outstretched arms

TOFFEE TIN, 1917

He keeps his boot polish in it
has done so by his recollection
for 60 years at least
he thinks he bought it
as a birthday present for his wife
though her face is as faint now
as the flavour of toffee after it is eaten
I tell him such boxes sell today
for twenty dollars or more in second-hand stores
he stares and shakes his head
as he slides the box back onto its shelf

Later we take him to the village snack-bar for coffee
he is known there and the waitresses respect
his hearing-aid his cane
they talk to him in that hearty voice
we all reserve for the very old
for children and foreigners
those quaint figures who appear
to decorate the edges of things
to fill the odd moments like this one
between lunch and suppertime
an old man sitting at a chrome table
fingers the paper packages of sugar
and even in this heat
his old man's sweater is buttoned
right up to the neck

FAMILY PORTRAIT

It begins with my brother's gift
of an old picture frame
picked up at an auction somewhere
and now this scene in the garden
the three of us dressed for a family portrait
my husband suddenly unsmiling
in an old suit of his uncle's
fingers the heavy watch chain in his vest
I smooth the folds of my long skirt
grow dreamy under the brim of an elaborate hat
and heavy loops of hair
while our son tugs at the wide bow
scratching his chin
grows sober under my brother's hands
arranging the angle of an elbow
the tilt of a head
we stiffen and recede into sepia
appear again above our fireplace
among the other ancestral photographs
yellowing on the mantle
staring down on our present selves
daily we grow less familiar
our faces vaguely reminiscent
of faces we think we remember
but assumed were dead
faces we have never seen
emerging at last
from the bone camera
behind our eyes

RENOVATING

You buy the place
thinking it will be easy
a few days spent stripping away
the old couple's hummingbird and ivy wallpaper
lifting up faded carpets
sanding the floors
but after four coats of white paint
darker colours still
shadow their way through
and the living-room
seems to sigh with disappointment
at your thin furniture
your lack of ornate picture frames

it takes months before
you understand what is expected
begin to accept
the limitations of other lives
like the layers
of thick dry paint on the woodwork
impossible to remove
stains on the bare floors
scratches worn places
become incidental as wrinkles or thumbprints

you learn to move
with a kind of dignity
through the high-ceilinged rooms
respecting those corners
where the light falls oddly
or alters when you turn your head
and at night
when the house mutters in its sleep
you think you hear
bits of your days echo

among the scraps of dream
old memories that hover in the dark
hear them on the edge of waking
as you turn
as the house settles again
begins to breathe easily
around you

SETTLING DOWN

Their lives
settle around them
slowly
like old houses
on stone foundations

daily
their habits harden
bricks interlocked

they seldom
clean the windows
opened so long
on one perspective
they have it memorized

Sometimes at night
the house creaks
they shift in their beds
dream
of waking in rubble
opened
to the sky

THE HOUSE OF OUR DREAMS

The house of our dreams
is heated by the sun
clean and silent as the future
it keeps us one with the ecology
and even the toilet makes compost
for the organic garden

In the house of our dreams
we return to the farmland
our parents left for the cities
to the old ways   homemade bread
jars of preserves in the pantry
hand-made dishes
and the scrubbed bare furnishings
of a dead generation
in the house of our dreams
we live unhaunted
among other people's ghosts

In the house of our dreams
even our children's names
are old and elemental
Judah River   Amy Snow
they thrive on brown rice lentils
Woody Guthrie
Bob Dylan

In the house of our dreams
it is a standing joke
that our children will turn out to be
bank managers
chartered accountants
but we do not believe this
we are as far from imagining this
as we are from the way our parents sit

even now in their highrises
their retirement bungalows
sit having coffee with friends
their tongues awkward around the names
of their grandchildren
and after they have said them
the way they smile
and stare in a kind of astonishment
at the still-warm cups
in their hands

Signs of the Former Tenant

Moving Away from the Past

Things you use; things you possess, and are possessed by, things you build with – bricks, words. You build houses with them, and towns, and causeways. But the buildings fall, the causeways cannot go all the way. There is an abyss, a gap, a last step to be taken.

– Ursula K. Le Guin

Nothing is ever the same as they said it was.
It's what I've never seen before that I recognize.

– Diane Arbus

RED LIGHT, GREEN LIGHT

Something about playing outdoors
in the long summer evenings after supper
the particular quality of the light then
how it seemed to round
and soften even the most heat-glazed afternoons
so that the memory of those games
– the grace of our bodies emerging from the awkward
tangle of an ordinary growing up
into the fluid movement of our play –
has the glow of a painting
by Christopher Pratt an adult's dream
of a lost time

The best game was
Red Light Green Light
the person who was it stood
at the side of the house
back turned against the others
poised at the garden's edge
ready to move
when the call began
green light green light green light
moving quietly forward
then *red light* and everyone stopped
freezing in mid-step
as the person who was it turned
to catch anyone who moved
I see Sharon You're it

This was a game we played
only in the evenings a game that belonged
to that particular light its way
of gathering the sounds of our playing
into itself

When you were it you could barely
hear the movements of the others
faint rustlings in the air behind you
fainter than your own fading voice
green light   green light   green light
the chant shivering away from you
half afraid to turn and waiting
for someone to spring from behind
grab you by the shoulders
Home Free   You're it again

Something about the way that light
was easing the day so slowly away
from us   the figure huddled
at the side of the house
growing smaller and smaller
as the distance from the garden's edge stretched
ahead until the sounds of our own feet
in the grass seemed to follow us
like invisible animals
and the voices of our mothers
drifted toward us
from another world
impossible to think of entering
the harsh yellow light   the improbable rituals
of toothbrushes and bedtime stories
green light   green light   green light

but even as we kept gliding dreamily
toward that sound
now fragile as the light around us
even then we were changing   stiffened
by our mothers' voices   their shrill
authority making the damp ground suddenly
cold to our bare feet   Sharon!
Right now!   I mean it!   *green light*
green light   Sharon!

the huddled figure turning then
larger for a moment   flash of white
limbs disappearing   the dark shape
of her mother in the porch light
bringing the night down darker
behind us   *g'night*
g'night

Something about that game and the particular
receding light drawing our voices
away with it   our footsteps almost soundless
in the hushed grey grass
as if the act of memory itself
were a kind of moving   a trick
of knowing when to turn and how
the way I walk through a summer's
evening now feeling my body soften
under a loose cotton dress
and the sound of my footsteps
making me turn and stop
and stand there   half surprised
to find myself alone
no other children poised in mid-step
leaning toward me

IN MY MOTHER'S FAVOURITE STORY

In my mother's favourite story
I am three years old
wearing a blue smocked dress
white ankle-socks and soft white shoes
it is the end of June   after dinner
and I am playing with my dolls
on the front porch while my parents
finish their coffee in the kitchen
my mother keeping an eye on me
through the screen door
she adds a bit more sugar to her cup
stirs   and looks out again to find
I've vanished
I am not on the porch where my dolls sit
complacently staring at nothing
I am not on the front lawn
not playing in the sandbox at the back
my father goes out to the edge of the sidewalk
and looks up and down the street
nothing
he begins to walk west crossing MacDonnell
which is not too busy at this time of day
and on up the next long block
past the TB sanitarium *(when I think of it*
now my mother will say *it still*
makes me shudder   the thought of all those
sick old men on the porch
spitting on the sidewalk)
he stops at Regent which is always crowded
cars moving steadily in both directions
there is no traffic-light   but an old woman
walking her dog says "Why yes, I did see
a little girl in a blue dress cross here
and you know I wondered, so tiny and …"
my father rushes out as brakes squeal

and two blocks later
he finds me still heading west
toward the banks of pink sunset clouds
"Ice cream" I tell him pointing at the sunset
"strawberry ice cream"
he carries me home crying
my arms outstretched over his shoulder
to the lost treat
home to where my mother sits
with her hand on the phone
ready to call the police
and then he runs to the corner store
for a gallon of strawberry ice cream
and long after my bedtime
the two of them hover around me
watching me eat

In my mother's favourite story
I am the child-hero of a thousand legends
moving through dangerous familiar streets
toward the vision no-one else can see
and always her telling of it weaves
around me like a net her hopes
her sinewy expectations it explains
me somehow accounts for the green dogs
and rainbow-coloured cats I drew in grade school
the conversations with fairies repeated
straight-faced at the dinner-table
and like all good myths it is a charm
against the darker aspects of the story
the pale grey men whose deaths
rasp in their chests and the blind shapes
of trucks looming toward the tiny figure
mingle in her mind with the nightmare
monsters the cruel eyes that kept us
both awake for years
you were always imaginative she tells me

and even now the story grows as I do
and its adult version is a woman
writing poems and drinking soup from chipped cups
not noticing the dishes piled for days
in a dirty sink   while her children
grow up untended and surprising
as flowers in a neighbour's garden

But in my mother's favourite story
I am rescued by my father
who becomes that legendary figure
striding through the hazards of my journey
to bring me home
like Alice and Dorothy and so many others
discovering the thing I sought
right there in my own ordinary house
so what can I tell her now   seeing the way
she has woven the story so well and kept
its charm around me for so long
how can I say that I remember nothing of the incident
that the tiny child in the blue smocked dress
and soft white shoes
seems as remote from me
as any fairy tale
that the treacherous streets of her journey
remain lost somewhere behind
the unexpressive face of this town I return to
only on visits   driving my car toward
my parents' house   the red bloom
of a sunset caught for a moment in my windshield
then disappearing as I turn a corner

I am not thinking of strawberry ice cream at all
though always at these moments
my mother's story flickers through my mind
the momentary gleam of a fish swimming through water
the bright skin of my childhood curling

away from me   though deep within my brain somewhere
the real event repeats itself in my cells
again and again the young child moves
through dangerous familiar streets
is rescued and returned
bur I am beyond her now   that tiny figure
and I would tell my mother that there are no charms
no words magical enough to fill
the silences that tighten in our throats
like dry coughs   I would have her know
all streets are treacherous and even the best
loved children forget the rules
about crossing with the light
but perhaps she knows this anyway
it's her story after all and she always
puts herself in   alone in the house
her hand on the telephone
and her eyes on the scattered toys
so easily abandoned
on the empty porch

STANLEY'S LADIES WEAR, CIRCA 1952

This is a country
where I have no authority
there is no toy department here
nor even the pleasure
of a red velvet dress
with a lace-trimmed collar
on a mannequin just my size
here the ladies sit
on wooden stools while salesgirls
show them gloves and silk scarves
the stools are as high
as the ones at Kresge's lunch-counter
but they don't spin
and my mother has told me twice now
not to touch the glass top of the display case

My mother is wearing her red hat
the one that makes her black hair
curl around the brim as crisply
as the hair on my favourite doll
when I told her this she laughed
and cupped her hands around my face
she has perfect hands
so soft they feel like wings
against my cheeks
and so small
that already the tip of my ring-finger
touches her wedding band
today she is buying gloves
and if I am patient and good
we will go for a soda afterward
but it is a long time
since the lady showed her the red pair
red as her hat   they fit so perfectly
I thought she would clap her hands

right there in the store
but instead she says
they are too dear
and now her lips have that thin
white line they get
when she is worried or cross

Near the back of the store
is a glass case full of fur collars
like the one my grandmother has
a fox with glass eyes
chasing his tail
around the top of her coat

I slip off my stool
and squat down to put my own face
closer to their pointy noses

When I stand up again
my mother has left the counter
and is walking toward the door
with a thin grey box in her hand
"Mommy," I call. "Mommy!"
but she does not stop
though a fat lady in a green coat
and a thin one in a brown jacket
turn toward the umbrella-stand
where two little girls are eating licorice
they do not look at me at all
though they answer to the name of "Mommy"
and now the store is full
of mothers with little girls
but mine is that woman in the red hat
striding toward the door
like someone who always
sets her own pace   someone who might have
other names   they beat

in my ears like wings   my tongue
tightens   it tries "Mrs. Wallace"
a cough that the woman opening the glass door
cannot hear   and then
my throat becomes a red noise "Betty!"
I scream at her "Betty, wait for me!"
and in the silence
her name makes she is there
above me   her lips
have that thin white line but
she takes my hand   we go
to Kresge's   there are explanations
I can't hear and in the grey box
are the red gloves
she tries them on for me
her hands swooping
like red birds
though she can't think
what my father will say
when we get home

GETTING THE WORDS FOR IT

O I admit that I
Hold to words
I hold them tight
I've known colder comfort
In the night
–Ferron

It came with the weather
July in southeastern Ontario
and the days soaking up heat
like a sponge I would have squeezed
if only my hands had been big enough
and if only I'd been younger or older
maybe it wouldn't have been so bad
having to rest in the afternoons
but I was eight and a half
and went to school all day when school was on
and never felt tired a tiny bit
"This is different," my mother said
"You need your strength; you never know."

And I didn't only that there was something
out there in the shimmering afternoon
that was dangerous
that crept up our street that summer
like the squash vines stretching in my father's garden
one of the Carmichael twins got it
and then the Sanderson boy who lived
across the corner half-way up the block
so I didn't really see what the men were carrying out
that morning when I went to call my kitten
only knew enough to feel ashamed later
my mother pale in the kitchen
and my father looking down at me
as if I'd said a bad word

(this was before the vaccine you understand
before the principal of your school could announce
between glee-club rehearsals and band practices
that grade nines would report to the gym at eleven
for their polio shots)

you can say it now and it rolls from your lips
as easily as any other word
but that wasn't what waited in my room
the night I complained of sore throat and headache
my parents' faces ballooning above
their voices sinking through the heat
pressed into my chest my legs
like huge moist hands   and then my doctor's
bony fingers tearing me from half-sleep
(our doctor walked with a crutch
and the sight of it leaning on my bedside table
sent me screaming to the far side of the bed
maybe he had it too   maybe I'd get it
from him   but what he had
was something from a war or an accident
you didn't talk about my father said
it wasn't the same)

It came with the weather
swollen and persistent as the heat
that held the city all that summer
until fall and school and new sweaters
diminished it to a few syllables
smooth and cool on our tongues again
leaving me to discover for myself
how every word has its climate
saying *fuck* out loud for the first time
in the car with my mother and learning what it meant
by the whiteness of her knuckles on the steering-wheel
and the whiter silence slowing the world
down   cars behind us blaring

like foghorns through the thickness of it
learning the smaller shifts
the intricate atmospheres
of *please* of *no* of *sorry*
learning how to hold each word
I used as my protection
from the seasons around it
(the word *flu* blowing its cold breeze
over my head and the doctor's hand
reaching for his crutch
dim shape of him in the doorway
grey cloth of his trousers
like a weary banner   flapping
around his legs)

CHRISTMAS, GRADE SIX

In grade five it didn't matter
the Christmas play
something to get through
before the holidays   now
we practise lines in secret
sing   gloria
where no-one is listening
wait for Friday morning
when Miss Fisher says
(as if it didn't matter at all)
"Gayle Scott will be the angel"

At recess the rest of us whisper
into tight knots   at rehearsal
flaunt the bright armour of shepherds' cloaks
against her white wings   long pale hair
make faces when she sings   giggle
behind our hands   wait patiently
for vengeance   'till Gayle Scott
has her hair permed   short tight curls
Miss Fisher's face goes red "Your hair! you cut
your hair!" and then her teacher voice
"Sharon will take your place. Sharon …"
tosses back long dark curls
moves centre stage
the rest of us silent
in shepherds' cloaks   bright
safe armour

THE HEROES YOU HAD AS A GIRL

The heroes you had as a girl
were always three grades ahead of you
taller than the boys in your own class
taller even than your brothers
and the layers of muscle ripening
under their thin shirts their jeans
made your palms itch
for something you didn't know how to explain
but wanted to   sitting with your girlfriends
in the hot dry grass
at the edge of the parking-lot
where all day Saturday they worked on their cars
hunched over the greasy mysteries of their engines
occasionally raising their heads
their eyes flicking
to where you were included
as part of the landscape

Sundays they practised more dangerous manoeuvres
till your eyes stung with the smell
of oil and burning rubber
and once they built arches of flaming
orange crates   you remember them spinning
through the air when one car missed
remember the screams that burned your throat
before you realized no-one was hurt
your voices fluttering like foolish birds
on the wild currents of their laughter

and now twenty years later the hero
who drove that car returns as unexpectedly
as the memory and just as out of place
you watch him study a display of bathroom fixtures
in the hardware department of Simpsons-Sears
he's grown fat and balding

and you think how easy it would be
to walk right over tap him
on the shoulder say *hello*
remember me and if he didn't
you could laugh it off
at least you've kept your figure
that's not what stops you now
though something does
and as he walks away
you can feel the dry grass biting
the backs of your legs the uncomfortable
angle of your knees as you sat just so
practising your own dangerous manoeuvres
not being noticed not noticing
the other girls forgetting their names
the shapes of their faces reddening in the sun
(though you remember those burning arches
your throat tightening again around those foolish screams)
you think you could explain it now
and that's what stops you
knowing you want nothing less
than for him to turn
peel off his shirt to show you
burn scars on his chest
and in the sullen landscape of his eyes
you want the faces of those girls
your own among them burning
brighter than any fire

AFTER THE DANCE

Before of course you went
to a friend's place
at least two hours ahead of time
locked in her room
sharing eye makeup and cigarettes
blowing the smoke out the window
so her mother wouldn't know

conferring with equal seriousness
about shades of lipstick and french kissing
you traded your slim wisdom
as freely as you traded sweaters or charm bracelets
you wouldn't have missed those hours
for the world even then you knew
these were the rituals that guided you
toward the real event
though once you got there you avoided
each other's eyes scanning the dance-floor
for the boys you'd giggled about
that too was understood clearly
and without words your girlfriends vanishing
as soon as he stepped forward

and after the dance while he waited outside
you collected your things from the cloakroom
where the ones who would walk home alone
lent you perfume straightened your collar
gestures you took for granted
like the simple confidence of knowing
that tomorrow there would be Cokes and long discussions
something so obvious
you didn't even think about it then
smiling as you walked away
the casual wave over your shoulder
as you took his arm

it's only now that memory
surprises you   knowing how many nights
you have sat in some woman's kitchen
a friend you haven't seen in months
who takes you in again gives coffee and Kleenex
while you cry over another man
who's hurt you
it's only now that image
humbles you somehow   the young girl
in a borrowed sweater   that smile
that nonchalant
wave

THAT STORY YOU TOLD

(For Liz Whynot & Linde Zingaro)

That story you told of the old woman
in your hometown who always walked
with her breasts thrust forward
swinging hips   her fingers toying
with a lock of hair *like a young girl*
who's been told how pretty she is you said
until that's all she thinks about. Only with her
it seemed as if she'd stopped
there somehow   stuck in a moment
of being admired till it froze her body
to this awkward posture, these continual
nervous tics. The only gestures that she knew
become grotesque and laughable.

That was the night we spoke
of our mothers and the stories we had
of the lives they'd led before they married
and became just that   only our mothers
in dirty aprons   damp hair flat
against their foreheads as they did the dishes
how those stories and the younger photographs
that showed them laughing
and beautiful haunted our girlhood
like fragile ghosts

All night we sat together
over a bottle of wine   our words rushing
toward each other   each thought
opening to the next so sure
of itself and moving as hands move
in their intricate intentions
pouring more wine or lighting a cigarette
no misses even though we were a little drunk

we had our futures plans
as glowing as our faces in the candlelight
till those old women faded
to figures in some myth
we'd read almost forgotten now
they seemed so far away
and yet sometimes
I think we haunt each other somehow
days when I'm late for work and rushing for the bus
and the old woman sweeping her walk on the corner
turns toward me with a startled half
expectant look blurred hands outstretched
as I run by
but mostly on slower mornings
rising from my lover's bed to stand
before a mirror touching my face my hair that radiant
reflection I think of how you stood that night
amidst our laughter mimicking
that old woman think of her too
standing as any woman stands before a mirror
reaching to that bright self
that lingers still
in the smooth glass
of her dreams

TUESDAY MORNING

Not this kitchen
but the one that maps
behind your eyes
its perspective of table-legs
and bottom drawers
the hem of your mother's skirt
a world of voices
resonant with meaning
and arms that carved
infallible gestures
in the air above you

like your grade-six history teacher
remember him   old
Hunchback Henderson
you called him   though
never to his face
yet you assumed somehow
he'd chosen his deformity
the way he chose the high stool
he used to reach the blackboard
how he could twist himself
to write and still turn on the slightest sound
his chalk whistling through air
at someone's forehead   always
accurate as radar
how for years he clung
to the underside of your imagination
like a troll
twisting his darkened powers
through your dreams

so that now
as you sit here
in your own kitchen among

dishes you chose yourself and the familiar
voices of your children
it comes upon you
like a revelation the thought
that he was merely an old man
desperate with pain
afraid of your whispers
the brutal thickness of your laughter

and for a moment something
in the kitchen shifts
as if the light from the window
had been split somewhere and the flat surfaces
it touches peel away
to where the adults of your childhood
even your parents flicker
like figures in an old movie
suddenly awkward fishmouths
gulping for words as their arms
clutch and falter
fade and

the kitchen settles again
you sit where you did a moment ago
hearing the hum of the refrigerator
the slow beats of the clock
and from outside
the voices of your children come
confident as sunlight
so that you know
without raising your eyes to the window
that they have climbed again
to the top of the apple tree
and against your warnings
your helplessness are
right now balancing
into the sky

BECOMING A GENERATION

Just the other day the babysitter
asked me if I knew anything about
something called Woodstock
she'd read about it somewhere
and I tried to tell her only
it got all mixed up with
exactly where I was when
I heard about Kennedy
and marching against the war
and Chicago in '68 and
how I cried when Janis Joplin died
my voice started shaking
and her face took on a look
that reminded me of the night
my father got into his stories
about riding trains in the '30s
only right in the middle of the one
about the winter he worked in the
logging camp he stopped and said
"that was the happiest winter of my life"
even my brother was embarrassed then
and changed the subject

Since then I've noticed
he ends with the bit about
the guy in the next bunk who
read the dictionary every night
and when he came out of the woods
in the spring landed a job
as a schoolteacher which is
a great story and a
good trick I must remember it
for next time

INSIDE OUT

A man I know whose father used to slap him
on the back of his head
when he put his elbows on the table
still knows the explicit taste of that humiliation
the saltiness of snot and held-back tears
that sting his tongue sometimes
when he sits down to dinner

this is not a memory
it's what another friend a woman
feels as ice in the pit of her stomach
when she's dressing for a party
cold as the telephone receiver
in her palm the boyfriend who never showed up
laughing at her drunkenly at one AM
and she's sixteen again
in a yellow formal staring
at the flecks of nailpolish the crusted rings
her coffee-cups have left
on the grey top of the kitchen table
it's not the recounting of childhood
I'm telling you about   the versions of it
handed out to friends when we return
like condescending ghosts who peer in
on the antics of the living
with futile "if only I had knowns" on their lips

not that at all it's the immediate
cramping in my stomach
when I see an african violet for example
that private mingling of shame and anger
tightening the cords in my neck
and strangling my tongue as I explain again
to Mrs Frederick my grade-three teacher
that what happened to them was an accident

and she says I'm a liar but
I'm not I'm not though Mrs Frederick
still thinks so and
it still matters

is this making any sense
try it this way
maybe you've noticed yourself that as you grow
older you take comfort in being the same
as your friends   calling yourselves a generation
comparing phases pleased to find
your children and theirs are the same age

and then one night a bunch of you
together at a party say and one of the men
gets a little drunk and enters a night
when he was thirteen camping with a friend
in a rickety pup-tent and hearing the racket
of a bear in the cooler they'd left outside
the two of them crouched in the swaying
tent ready to fight it off with jack-knives

and maybe you've noticed then how this man's
voice (a man with sons of his own to keep
from danger) how his voice cracks and the hand
with the jack-knife in it flails above his head
as if the process of the body's changing
every seven years had suddenly reversed and speeded up
the cells returning to him that
pure fearlessness   pure terror
haven't you felt it yourself
in whatever moment
chooses you like that
a moment you thought you'd left forever
carrying the person you were then
like a half-tamed animal tenderly in your arms

haven't you felt yourself
surrendered to the starkness of that instant
when you become the child again
unique and alone as only children are
staring out at the world
from the stubborn depths of it

TOWARD MORNING

I wake from the recurring dream
a woman crying
her eyes dark with the knowledge
of her own death
and moving through the darkness
of the dreaming house
I come downstairs   make tea
and drink it in my favourite chair
while the dream hesitates
along the curve of lamplight
sinks to the deeper corners of the room

around me I can almost hear
my plants growing their own way
through the night   and beyond them
in his room upstairs my son
steps earnestly through dreams
that leave their mark each morning
the strips of muscle beginning
to mold themselves across his chest and back
the determined bones emerging
from the baby fat

I think of the man I love
perhaps he is still awake
in his house in another part of the city
sitting alone listening to his stereo
but his eyes have the look of someone
who dreams himself far away
and the stubborn cadence of his thought
following the music to a new job in another city
has nothing at all to do with me

I look down at my hands
and they occur somehow as independent beings
secure in their strict knowledge of tangible things
their dumb memories visible
in the palmlines   the scar
on my one finger obstinate as the knife
that created it although the childhood incident
is gone now
cannot be recalled

already and without my willing it
my hands prepare for the future
the flesh around my knuckles loosens
the veins on the backs grow sinewy
as an old woman's

all changing is a kind of dying

I close my eyes and see the faces of my friends
fine lines around their mouths
grey hair at the temples
women my own age who seem to inhabit their bodies
with such an adult grace
I can hardly believe
they might sit as I do now
amazed at how my body slides
so easily away
from what I think I am   the young girl
stretching within me   still
waiting to grow up

and yet they do

I switch off the light   rise
rinse my tea-cup and leave it on the counter
it will be here tomorrow   oddly reminiscent
an old relic from some older journey

forgetting the fingers that have touched it
as even now the woman who places it here
turns casually away and gliding beyond me
starts toward morning
through the still
sleeping rooms

I LIKE TO BELIEVE MY LIFE

I like to believe my life
is slowly tidying itself
finishing things up
like a good novel
that's what I think I like
about the past
the way it seems to smooth itself around me
a favourite shirt I've worn
for years until it's comfortable
as skin and just as certain (though
what it does without me   forgetting
my smell   the shape of my shoulders
and growing its own changes in the back
of the closet is another matter)

meanwhile the present
muddles around me
cluttered with scraps of toast
the greasy bits of egg still
clinging to the dumb white plates
the present's always sighing
and vaguely dissatisfied while I
keep trying to patch it up
re-doing last week's argument
with the landlord a dozen times
in my mind or writing imaginary letters
to someone I never slept with
but wish I had

and only last week
a man who was my lover once
called from the airport
in town for a few hours
suggesting dinner
for old times' sake

he hadn't changed a bit
though if this were a proper story
I'd have given him some wrinkles
an interesting scar   the suggestion
of some deep sadness in his eyes
I know he'd do the same for me

as it was we made do
with what we had   opening ourselves
to each other like story-books
appearing in a few well-chosen anecdotes
like characters from someone else's life
and later back at my place
we made love as casually
as those who have been apart
for only a few hours

as if even here
there are not those tinier changes
so many delicate layers of skin
we must move through
before the rediscovery
of an earlobe   the particular scent
of someone's hair

he left before dawn
to catch his plane and
must have sent me flowers
from the airport
they arrived that morning
roses of course   red ones
perfectly formed and unapologetic
as roses usually are
though I suppose if this
were a proper story
they'd have wilted in an hour
or been pressed into a bible

to be found years later by my daughter
something like that   but having no use
for metaphors they lasted
about as long as any roses
then scattered themselves
abruptly over the table

all week I've been waiting
for them to become something
for the night they grew from
to tidy itself somehow
but there's just this
almost unconscious movement
of my hand brushing the greying petals up
with an old envelope
an action as indefinite
as the wave I'd give a friend
I expected to see in a day or so
the half-turn from my doorway
as she drove off
a little too quickly
a little too carelessly
out of sight

LIKE THE TELEPHONE

Like the firm click of the telephone receiver
that puts three thousand miles between us
the stiff set
of your shoulders   your determined
not-to-look-back stride away
from me here in this airport
(like all those other airports   bus depots
train stations) I seem to keep standing in
watching you go

not at all like the movies I grew up on
lovers moving through prolonged farewells
to appropriate music   the camera playing
on each face in turn   each shift of emotion
registered in closeup

I can't even see your face and now
other people crowd between us
to them you're just another man
at the boarding gate with nothing to connect you
to the woman who stands here
fumbling for her cigarettes

already   something has been
altered (the match flares in my hand
and sharp smoke bites against tears
in my throat) I look up
to the back of your head receding
between a man with a guitar
a woman carrying a small child
so that even if I called you
now and you turned
and waved   even if I
were leaving you here
it would still be like those nights

on the phone our voices stretching
always coming up
against the last goodbye
knowing there isn't time
for whatever it is we must
say before our words dissolve
into the hum of wires
other conversations eager
to begin

Between Words

FREEZE FRAME

Imagine this kitchen
as a scene for a film
the remains of breakfast
scattered on the table
light falling in precise angles
over plates and sugar-bowl
a man and a woman sit
over coffee   hands curled
around brown mugs
one of them has just spoken
not about the weather
the day's headlines but
something that holds them
for a moment – the exact
moment when you enter –
suspended

the words are not important
because you know (this being
a film) that whatever happens
next will carry the force of
the words forward   will be
the significant gesture   his hand
reaching to her cheek perhaps or
closing a fist on the table
maybe her sudden rising and a door
like Ibsen's door banging shut
a gesture that implies
the weeks they have spent together
years   all that has been said
other mornings over breakfast or
left unspoken nights as they turned to sleep

it will be the high point of the film
but for now the camera concentrates
on the moment that precedes it
films this scene in the kitchen
again and again   a freeze frame
of the two of them sitting there
and as you enter
you can see yourself
in a moment like this one
but now for the first time
stilled as they are
you know precisely
how that split second
stretches – the camera
whirring behind you –
how the words spill and spread
slowly through the space between them
thicken in their eyes

and you understand then
how the next action   the gesture
that seems so simple so
spontaneous must move
through this stillness
these years of words and answers
as the arm of someone drowning
moves through water
heavy with the act
of pulling the body up
the scene caught over
and over the camera whirring
and this gesture upon which
everything depends
moving as that arm moves
to the surface of the water
shattering in the
clear air

A SIMPLE POEM FOR VIRGINIA WOOLF

This started out as a simple poem
for Virginia Woolf   you know the kind
we women writers write these days
in our own rooms
on our own time
a salute   a gesture of friendship
a psychological debt
paid off
I wanted it simple
and perfectly round
hard as an
egg   I thought
only once I'd said egg
I thought of the smell
of bacon grease and dirty frying-pans
and whether there were enough for breakfast
I couldn't help it
I wanted the poem to be carefree and easy
like children playing in the snow
I didn't mean to mention
the price of snowsuits or
how even on the most expensive ones
the zippers always snag
just when you're late for work
and trying to get the children
off to school on time

a straightforward poem
for Virginia Woolf   that's all
I wanted really
not something tangled in
domestic life the way
Jane Austen's novels tangled
with her knitting her embroidery
whatever it was she hid them under

I didn't mean to go into all that
didn't intend to get confessional
and tell you how
every time I read a good poem
by a woman writer I'm always peeking
behind it trying to see
if she's still married
or has a lover at least
wanting to know what she did
with her kids while she wrote it
or whether she had any
and if she didn't if she'd chosen
not to or if she did did she
choose and why   I didn't mean
to bother with that
and I certainly wasn't going
to tell you about the time
my best friend was sick in intensive care
and I went down to see her
but they wouldn't let me in
because I wasn't her husband
or her father   her mother
I wasn't family
I was just her friend
and the friendship of women
wasn't mentioned
in hospital policy

or how I went out and kicked
a dent in the fender of my car
and sat there crying because
if she died I wouldn't be able
to tell her how much I loved her
(though she didn't and we laugh
about it now) but that's what got me
started I suppose   wanting to write
a gesture of friendship

for a woman for a woman writer
for Virginia Woolf
and thinking I could do it
easily   separating the words
from the lives they come from
that's what a good poem should do
after all and I wasn't going to make excuses
for being a woman   blaming years of silence
for leaving us
so much to say

This started out as a simple poem
for Virginia Woolf
it wasn't going to mention history
or choices or women's lives
the complexities of women's friendships
or the countless gritty details
of an ordinary woman's life
that never appear in poems at all

yet even as I write these words
those ordinary details intervene
between the poem I meant to write
and this one   where the delicate faces
of my children   faces of friends
of women I have never even seen
glow on the blank pages
and deeper than any silence
press around me
waiting their turn

WOMAN SITTING

Somewhere right now a woman
sits in the silence of her kitchen
the silence her family leaves
when they brush past her into the day
intent on their own plans
and as she sits there
her hands shaking a little around
the coffee cup the cigarette
a dream comes back to her

in the comfortable dark
of her own living-room
she finds she can move things
with her eyes   it's fun at first
the way a heavy chair
slides easily from one wall
to the other   tables dangle
from the ceiling   lamps
swirl drunken arcs
in every corner
then
the darkness splits wide
open walls and ceilings
pulse and she can't stop
the liquid shift but just
as she feels herself about
to plunge   she touches
on the rim of waking
shrill voices of her children
demanding breakfast
clean underwear

But right now
in the quiet kitchen
in the silence of her family's leaving
she feels again
that moment of the dream
shifting away from her
feels it as something present
in the house   concealed
somewhere and the house
hardening against her
stubborn as a child
caught in a lie

feels it in the empty
spaces left by
her children's growing
and in the thicker silences
that sometimes clench like fists
beneath her husband's words

and through all that
she hears it
closing on the sounds of her day
the way grey earth in a dry season
soaks up the light thin rain

a woman
sitting in that kind of silence
with sunlight falling
through the dirty windowpane
to spill itself like smoke
around her

THE LOST DREAMS

… (the unconscious of the young mother – where does it entrust its messages, when dream-sleep is denied her for years?)
– Adrienne Rich, Of Woman Born

Awakened by her son's cry
she imagines her lost dreams
distributing themselves
among the neighbours
imagines the banker across the street
dreaming he dances barefoot
in a field of flowers
the retired schoolteacher next door
moaning as she turns toward
a gold and honeyed lover
but in the morning
they nod over their hedges
complacent as the sunshine
and she knows that at dinnertime
the kitchen counter will begin to crack
before her eyes
the potatoes she peels
will cry out like hurt children
and tonight her son
will scream again at beetles
slimy and four feet long
her dreams loose in the household
twisting themselves any way
but out

ALL THAT UNEASY SPRING

All that uneasy spring
we worked in our gardens
as soon as the earth was warm
we planted onions and peas
impatiens in the shade of our hedges
and marigolds in fiery rows along the walks
we set the seedlings out to harden
under sheets of glass
each of us looking up occasionally
to see the other women
in their yards   a series
of mirrored reflections   then
someone would wave from her kitchen
and we'd stop for coffee
leaving our mudcaked shoes
on the steps outside

And all that uneasy spring
our gossip came in whispers
like rumours from another land
divorces and custody disputes
how Anne's husband had kidnapped
her children from school
and Sharon had simply
left one afternoon and not come back
not even called

After the gardens were in
we washed the windows
repainted the lawnchairs
sent the drapes out to be cleaned
and at four
when the children arrived from school
we started the barbecues
scented our wrists

the cool drinks always ready
and the steaks just right
when our husbands pulled in the drive

But all that uneasy spring
when we lay in the dark
under crisp fresh sheets
the things we couldn't say
licked like flames
behind our eyes   our houses
were burning down   our children
screamed and sometimes our own voices
woke us surfacing through layers
of smoke to where our fingers touched
our husbands' bodies cool
and confident beside us
and awake then in that
uneasy dark we would remember
our morning conversations the sounds
of our voices coming back to us
suddenly precious even the smallest details
dirt-stained fingernails
the tiny lines that crinkled
white in sunburned skin
so that turning toward sleep
again we saw each other
standing in those hopeful gardens
while at our feet
the plants burst
dreamlike
from the slow dark ground

BETWEEN WORDS

(For Carole)

Because you so often think of her as
starched white she suddenly seems
smaller now
sitting across from you
in jeans and grey sweater
a beer in her hand and her voice barely
loud enough to reach you
over the noise of the jukebox
the voices of other people in the bar

You think you've known her
a long time and once in a while
you run into her like this
it's February and she's telling you
that this is the month
when all the women seem to come
from the hard bare farms
into the city for their yearly babies

Children themselves really she says
why some of them are only eighteen
maybe twenty and this will be
their fourth their fifth
they're always blond with pale
blue eyes pale skin
and something quiet about them
slow   slow-witted you'd think
but it's not that it's more
as if the way they think
is a kind of moving

as if they have to move
through the spaces
in between the words
do you know what I mean

She shrugs and lights a cigarette

Their husbands make up for it
though   God   they're old enough
to be their fathers   toothless
smelly old men   they just
drop them with their suitcases
and go off in these battered trucks
the other kids piled in beside them
and two days later three at the most
they're back to pick them up
and that's it
they're gone and you know for sure
half of them don't have running
water even   nothing
and you wonder really
where they do go

You know those times
when you drive along the highway
and you see a home   imagine living
there   imagine what the rooms are like
even if you've never been inside
you know you just know
well what I'm trying to say
is that wherever they go
is not like that
and scarier somehow

When I was in surgery
it was the smell that bothered me
even on my days off

I could smell blood or something
I kept trying to wash it off
afraid my husband or the kids
would notice
but this has to do with the eyes
and waking up at night and
those pale blue eyes
just there   not
saying anything not showing
anything   just

Her voice trails off
and you sit there
thinking of those pale blond
women   the pale earth
of their farms closing around
them   the two of you
knowing your lives
are shaped somehow by things
you can't touch
and shivering a little
in the stubborn silences
that grow
between the words

SIGNS OF THE FORMER TENANT

Whatever she did all day
it wasn't housework and
the lady downstairs says
the kids were always filthy
it takes me a day to remove
their fingerprints from the walls
and hours of scrubbing before
the tub gives up its dead-cell scum
and the oven is free of grease
even the smell is stubborn
windows open for days against
dirty diapers and stale food

The place is liveable now at least
though some things can't be fixed
the broken latch on the bedroom door
and the worn pattern of the tile
from the kitchen sink to the front window
where just at eye-level
faint smudges cling
like breath clouds
sobs imprisoned in glass

SIGNS OF THE FORMER TENANT II

An elderly man knocks at your door
one night while you are having dinner
and asks to see the place he lived
here years ago when he was no older
than your young lad there   lived here
with his mother just after his father left
he hasn't been back since and you wouldn't believe
how much the neighbourhood has changed
though he recognized the house at once and is pleased
to find the dark wood panelling still
in the dining-room and the built-in hutch
where his mother kept the family china
till his father came and took it away
of course it's different now they've built
that addition on the house next door
it spoils the view from the bay window
but the morning light would be the same
he used to play with the rainbows it made
when it shone through the beveled glass
at the top   oh yes it's lovely
you tell him as he keeps on standing there
while your family fidgets with the cold food
and you wish he'd leave or at least not notice
the scuff-marks your kids have made on the floors
the smell of baked fish in the hallway

we nestle in each other's lives
like spoons   the touch of them
not quite so solid perhaps
but just as definite

each time you move to a new
place you fill in other people's
spaces like the blank white squares
their pictures leave on the grey walls

you always have to deal with what
they leave behind   the bottles and coat-hangers
poking out of empty closets into
your light   the mail that keeps
arriving despite your constant calls
to the post office and all the time
somewhere someone else is standing
in your old kitchen laughing at the colour
of the cupboards or trying to piece together
a story from the odd stains
on your bathroom wall

even in a brand-new place
the smoothest paint contains
the workman's plans for Sunday and remembers
the lunchtime conversations   union politics
or last night's fight with the wife

we nestle in each other's lives
like lovers   spoon-shaped curve
of their bodies as they drift toward sleep
and even when we dream ourselves   alone
and far away we bump against
some small reminder of what we are
left with   live within

ISOLATED INCIDENT

What matters
is that she didn't say anything first
didn't yell "Shut up" or "Stop it"
didn't even shake the kid
just reached out and
slapped him   hard
across the face
right here in the crowded check-out line
at the Dominion Store
the raw fact of her hand
cutting the air so fast
it didn't give you time to turn away
no words to warn you anyhow
the way words usually do
the way you use them every day
scanning the newspaper headlines
for the safer articles
or knowing what people to avoid
on the street by the way they
mumble to themselves
giving you time to move
beyond their reach before they
try to grab your sleeve and pull you in
to wherever it is their words take them

And even now   the red mark
swelling on the pale fat flesh
like a kind of signature
is not enough
you can't read it
as you do old scars
on a stranger's face
signs of some isolated incident that happened
somewhere else   leaving you free
to arrange the details as you choose
or not

What matters
is the raw fact of her hand
and how its sudden entry
into your world strips it
down to that
unprotected meeting of two lives
from which nothing
not the dry-grass murmurs
of the women beginning around you
nor the determined click as the cashier
pushes the bar to send the groceries
into their crisp brown bags
not even the child's cry
rising now too late and
impossibly fragile
can ever totally
reclaim you

SPACES

It's Saturday and across the street
the man with the tidy house
is cutting down his poplar "Filthy
trees" he tells me "they're weeds
really and in the fall it's terrible
the way they drop things
all over the lawn"
Later one of his friends comes over in
a fancy truck with a winch on the back
and they pull the stump out   fill in the
hole and then his wife brings out
a polyethylene marble-effect bird-bath
($3.99 at Canadian Tire) filled with
petunias and plants it
on the bare spot
By two the yard's all cleaned up and
everybody's having a beer
the radio playing commercials
that float out over the yard
so comfortably that even the birds are quiet
and the remaining trees
thrive on the sound

and around the corner the Italian
with the limp he got in some
prisoner-of-war camp is planting
cabbages and beans in his front yard
no bigger than my bathroom
he's got fifteen tomato plants
and he tells me you can grow
anything with enough manure
his hands shape the memory
of last year's zucchini
huge as fire-hydrants
spilling over his front yard

while five miles from the city
there are farms still worked
by horses and dirt roads where
all day kids stand holding out
buckets of berries to
passing cars and on up
north of No. 7 stories drift down
from Ompah   Plevna
of a woman whose father
sold her to a man
for a sack of winter potatoes
it never makes the papers
but here in the city
it's 3 o'clock and there's
a wedding in the park two blocks over
"Portuguese" my neighbour tells me

there's at least 3 bridesmaids
2 flower-girls and the bride herself
surrounded by roses ornamental
shrubs and a ring of kids
drawn from the baseball diamond
and after it's all over
adolescent boys on bicycles
swoop down on the girls
who wait with careful disinterest
for their handful showers
of grass and
leftover confetti

meanwhile the man with the tidy house
has left for the evening and his kids
are having a party   the porch
ripples with denim and the smell
of marijuana swims out
over the street the other houses
are opening their secrets   someone's fighting

in the kitchen and someone else is
singing to a baby   beer bottles get
opened and ice clinks
in a glass   while over our heads
the sky is full of metal
space junk disintegrates
and sinks through astounded
spaces   splashing
down on a desert
somewhere
without hitting
anyone

INVASIONS

Sometimes it happens quickly
an ambulance siren slicing
the silence of the street
to stop outside the Gibson place
and the torn grey look
on Mr Gibson's face
as they bring his wife out
on a stretcher and help him
staggering a little in
beside her

everyone else
on this block of elderly couples
watches

an event
that marks their time
as clearly as a calendar
for weeks   each day
in every conversation
takes this instant
as its reference point

In this neighbourhood where
they have lived for over fifty years
each change is an invasion
though usually it's more indefinite
careless as dandelions discarded
toys that sprout on our front lawn
pushing aside their older memories
of Mrs Tait's meticulous shrubs
the shifts no instrument can measure
how a child's ball breaking
a rose bush hurts them
almost as much as the news

that the family moving in
on the corner are Pakistani

In spring when the sewers broke
and the city tore the street apart
replacing them   that too
was an event and everyone
stood on their sidewalks watching
for a week it was something
to talk about   the noise
and how the dust stuck
to your lips   the petals
of peonies   it was so
definite the progress
of machinery chewing its way
along the block and out of sight
leaving them still there
at last   even the shock
of the young women working alongside
the men to flag the cars down
even that only a memory
now the pavement's
smooth again   the days
lengthen into evenings
when they sit on their porches
watching the quiet street
as they always have
till we go past returning
from some errand with our noisy
children our bewildering
helloes that leave them groping
through a labyrinth of memories
for names   we're almost at our door
before we hear them
calling after us   their voices
quiver slightly in the air

as if they lean toward us in an eagerness
to make us hear
still there
still greeting us
despite whatever closes in
haphazardly around them

THE COUNTRY OF OLD MEN

They bring their silence with them
it stiffens against traffic sounds
and spreads itself over the shaved grass
of the bowling-green   holds them
to narrow parallels   the ball's course
sparse efficiency of pitch and follow-through
the terse exchange of scores and the weather
by which they measure out the months
between winters and the return
to their tidy houses   wives

They will keep track of each other
in the general way of barbershop and supermarket
will learn that Mr Wilson lost his wife in December
but not that in January he went
hatless among the neighbours
embarrassing the old couples
who asked if he were selling the house
and the young ones who stared politely
from half-opened doors
In April it will be noted
that his house is for sale
and his marriage in May
to a vague widow in her sixties
with a place of her own in the next block
will be marked by the slightest nod
and the comment that it's hard
for a man to manage on his own

In June when he returns
to the bowling-club
they will nod as he joins them
standing for a moment
to inspect the green
before they move off to their places

to linear paths
the occasional click
of wood
on wood

THE EDGE

He doesn't look that different
from other men his age
the way his hair curls on his collar
and the faded jeans he wears
T-shirt in summer   down jacket
for colder weather
you'd never notice him in a crowd
except that on the streets
he keeps close to the curb
away from the shop-window promises
and the towers of perfumed secretaries
he walks slowly
keeping his eyes on the edge
of the street where occasional coins
the careless nickels and quarters flash
like tiny fish in the dark litter
of leaves and dirty paper

He has a room on an old street
and the neighbours there know him
as polite but quiet   they talk about
how he spends his days
finds money enough to live on
though of course he must have made
much more before   why he was
the best mechanic in the area
could listen to your car
for a minute the slightest knock
enough to tell him what was wrong
as if he had a map of every engine down
to the tiniest screw and wire
right there in his head
now he can't even drive
after what happened
it's like whole parts of his brain

don't connect any more words he
can't remember or simple things
like how to operate a cigarette machine
you'd think the doctors could do something for him
but he seems to like it this way

Steps balanced on the curb
and the eyes tensed waiting
for the flicker that pulls the hand
down to the precise weight of thin metal
between two fingers   gestures so fine
that no-one notices at all really
except maybe just at dusk when the light
sharpens the branches of trees and the voices
of children playing in the streets
when he walks carefully back to his room
and the woman next door is lifting a casserole
from the oven and turns to see him framed
in her window just as she feels
the heat cut through her oven mitt
or her husband opens the door
for the evening paper and
seeing him there is glad
for the hard curve of the doorknob
in his palm

WHETHER YOU EXPECT IT OR NOT

it will happen
you will be watching
the late-night news
there will be a knock at the door
you will open it to the woman up the street
her face bleeding
she will tell you her husband is drunk
and has beaten her
and she is afraid to go back
but what about the kids
you will make tea and suggest
that she phone the police
but she says he'll kill her
he's on parole already
she thinks he might have a gun
and you will keep watching the window
while she tells you she is
four months gone with her third
and if she had the money
she'd go back to her family
in Italy because she knows
he is sleeping with her best friend
she will go on drinking tea
and smoking and talking
till all the other lights on the street go out
and the pictures on the TV fade
the empty screen opening
into your living-room
your kitchen   the bedroom
where your children sleep
into the whole dark sleeping street
of hedges and garbage-cans
houses living-rooms
TV screens opening
like mouths

THE WOMAN IN THIS POEM

The woman in this poem
lives in the suburbs
with her husband and two children
each day she waits for the mail and
once a week receives
a letter from her lover
who lives in another city
writes of roses   warm patches
of sunlight on his bed
Come to me he pleads
I need you and the woman
reaches for the phone
to dial the airport
she will leave this afternoon
her suitcase packed
with a few light clothes

But as she is dialing
the woman in this poem
remembers the pot-roast
and the fact that it is Thursday
she thinks of how her husband's face
will look when he reads her note
his body curling sadly toward
the empty side of the bed

She stops dialing and begins
to chop onions for the pot-roast
but behind her back the phone
shapes itself insistently
the number for airline reservations
chants in her head
in an hour her children will be
home from school and after that
her husband will arrive

to kiss the back of her neck
while she thickens the gravy
and she knows that
all through dinner
her mouth will laugh and chatter
while she walks with her lover
on a beach somewhere

She puts the onions in the pot
and turns toward the phone
but even as she reaches
she is thinking of
her daughter's piano lessons
her son's dental appointment
Her arms fall to her side
and as she stands there
in the middle of her spotless kitchen
we can see her growing
old like this
and wish for something anything
to happen we could have her go
mad perhaps and lock herself
in the closet crouch there
for days her dresses withering
around her like cast-off skins
or maybe she could take
to cruising the streets at night
in her husband's car
picking up teenage boys
and fucking them in the back seat
we can even imagine
finding her body
dumped in a ditch somewhere
on the edge of town

The woman in this poem offends us
with her useless phone and the persistent
smell of onions we regard her as we do
the poorly calculated overdose
who lies in a bed somewhere
not knowing how her life drips
through her drop by measured drop
we want to think of death
as something sudden
stroke or the leap
that carries us over the railing
of the bridge in one determined arc
the pistol aimed precisely
at the right part of the brain
we want to hate this woman
but mostly we hate knowing
that for us too it is
moments like this
our thoughts   stiff fingers
tear at again and again
when we stop in the middle
of an ordinary day and
like the woman in this poem
begin to feel
our own deaths
rising slow within us

The Cancer Poems

Hodgkins Disease: a chronic disease with lympho-reticular proliferation of unknown cause that may be present in localized or disseminated form.

– *Merck Manual, 334*

DIAGNOSIS

Later she would remember the day
as white snowdrifts piled by the roadside
drifting across her windshield
and the doctor's crisp white paper
words piled on his desk
tissue *lymph nodes* *white blood cells*
piled
and drifting

EXPLORATORY

The anaesthetist slips something silent
through her veins
and the light above grows large
as the sun swirls and shatters
little lights behind her eyes
"Just relax now
there's a good girl"

And there was a little girl
who had a little curl
blond curls   blue eyes
fat red cheeks
such a pretty little girl
cried the ladies
pretty on the outside
sniffed her mother   but
a bad girl underneath
handsome is as
handsome does

Later awake in the darkened room
she imagines the bright laboratory
the microscopes
hears again her doctor's
talk of cells   his
cautious optimism
but closing her eyes
sees still the place
where blood swirls
matted hair around
a face shaped

to her mother's words
drumming
the face
etching itself
still
deeper

CORN-HUSK DOLL

In the days that followed
she watched them
a curious onlooker
in the x-ray room the lab
where they checked her blood
saw the scars from
their exploratory operations
etch themselves across her flesh
and how even crowsfeet
wrinkles seemed to deepen
her body cracking around
whatever was loose within it
like the corn-husk dolls
she'd seen in craft shops
silk hair and jeweled eyes
gay red cheeks but
no mouth

a brittle doll
in a pale-blue nightgown
the silence rising
through the pores of her skin
her sequined
eyes

FIRST DREAM

In an old section of the city
in the window of an empty shop
a book
draws her
in bells tinkle
at the door
the old man refuses to sell
and just as
their voices rise
another tinkle of the bell
brings what she knows
before turning
has been following
all day a figure
faceless and cold
touch of fingers on her wrist
eyes
black tunnels
draw her to
their edge as
with the other hand
he offers the book
"but it was mine all along"
she struggles too late
to say before
the opening
of his eyes
stops her
fills
her mouth

SECOND DREAM

A house with arched windows
spiral staircase

In one of the rooms
something waits

Corners shape themselves
to arms reaching
out she races
up the staircase
along halls footsteps
follow pounding her heart
pounding opens a door
the wrong one her way
blocks
as something
reaches for her turns
a man's soft face
and hands
offering
biscuits
wine

TREATMENT

For the doctors it seemed
simple as an old war
even the drug they used
mechlorethamine
a derivative
of mustard gas dripped
into her veins
as she lay
arms outstretched
the chemical burning into her
an older ritual
given a new name
demons to be exorcised
a witch in need of cleansing
And somehow it was
all familiar the white tiles
and bright paint of the clinic
not unlike the kitchen
where her mother stood
and the doctors' voices
reminiscent *easy now*
there's a good girl no tears
now big girls don't cry
or yell

not unlike her own kitchen
smells of breakfast and
her hands clenched around
her coffee cup
as the voices of her children
husband pulled at her
claws against her skin
till she shaped herself to
the good mother
the perfect wife rising

to find mittens neckties
her smile stitched across
whatever rose in her throat
and the coffee in her cup
thickened

So she told no-one of her dream
witch dream where she shrank
to the size of a snail
and journeyed the warm seas
of her blood   found her womb
fragrant with moss and ferns
or how in her chest beyond
the place where her heart
shone like a blue jewel
something dark and
colder than silence
unfolded its deathscent
mingling with the smell
of ferns
didn't tell   didn't tell
how she rushed out
through her mouth and
forced it shut around
this double blossoming
while the doctors talked
of healing   her flesh
loosened and her hair
came away
in handfuls

SNOW WHITE

Days grew liquid
light from her window
flowed around her bed
where it hardened
brittle as glass
Snow White in her glass coffin
while overhead like pale blossoms
faces bob and press
  does it hurt
  are you getting better
  are you   alright
  alright ALRIGHT
She watches their mouths
gasping as they thrust
the word at her
sees how their eyes
glide anxiously toward
the dark forest shapes
prowling the edges of their vision
the possibility of other answers
than the ones
their mouths demand

she thinks of Snow White
was there a moment (the sound
of hoofbeats in the distance
the prince arriving) a moment
when she felt the things
forced down so long rise
in her throat   imagined
shattering the glass
into the dwarfs' faces
with her fists   beating
at her step-mother did she
imagine this just

before the prince reached
down and gathered her
to a safer
more familiar
ending

THIRD DREAM

She sits fishing
in a boat at the centre
of a grey lake
hooks and reels in
a dead body
vomit rising
chokes her screams as
the thing twitches
twists into
a monkey in cap and jacket
turning cartwheels
on the bow
and on a silver flute
blows notes to
silver bubbles
float and loom
along the shore
lights
of a magic city

FOURTH DREAM

An old house again
or prison
her fingers white slugs
feel their way along damp walls
toward music voices
a dance she must attend
but in the garden
just as she comes in sight of
paper lanterns
an old man under a bare tree
stops her

She sits with him
on cold ground
leans toward the music
he is trying to tell her
something but she cannot
hear "here" he says
"here" and she turns to
his face blazing
and the tree above their heads
all sudden crystal
shines with leaves and fruit
flashing like prisms
birds of blown glass
sing and
radiant as the tree
she spins all night
in the brilliant shapes
of their song

SORCERESS

Dying made everything possible
the way the morning sun
tipped her breakfast tray
and the day rose slowly
shaped to her hands like fresh bread

below her the house moved dreamlike
through its own waking
the sounds of breakfast
voices of husband children
lapped gently against her closed door
and receded
left her to herself
neither wife nor mother
nor adult
she lived like the first inhabitant
of a new city and gathered
its magic for her own

she wore her dying
like a sorcerer's cape
and powerful with wishes
disguises she became
the mad wife in the attic
the heartless step-mother
explored again
the pure anger of childhood
cups shattered at the wall
the pieces swirling
in her screams

Daily she was child and sorceress
clothed in forbidden shapes of herself
and daily she learned
the source of her magic

saw in the mirror how
she grew more beautiful
grew vast and complex
became the city
she inhabited

And returning to the house
laid out for her like a holiday
she saw for the first time
exactly how the light lay
on the kitchen table
how the beauty of her children's faces
felt sharp as birth pains
and the days then glistened
with games
the stories her children brought
their wishes lay in her hands
like the bright dreams
of circus monkeys
and sometimes in the evenings
watching the warm shape
of her husband's hands
as he poured wine
she would spin again
in her radiant dance
and breathless see
across the water-shimmering room
the wine's ripe crystal fruit
held like a wish
at the delicate tip
of her reaching

REMISSION

Slowly the days took shape once more
separated themselves
into hours minutes
friends called less often
and when they did they talked about
the weather or the government
she began to do her own housework
and finally
smiling over the latest lab report
the doctors gave her a schedule for
three-month checkups and for the moment
let her go

outside the clinic
she sits in the parking-lot
as the first few snowflakes
gather in the late afternoon
on the street figures
clench themselves like fists
around the cold
and watching them
she imagines how
the flat winter light
lies on the top of her kitchen table
the edges of chairs
the faces of her family
almost apologetic in the way
it hardens on the surfaces it touches
as if to shape them in its own cold
and she herself stands
at the stove preparing supper
familiar as milk
as if the radiant witch of her dreams
the mad wife the cruel step-mother
even death itself were houseguests

departed now for trains and airports
unable to enjoy themselves here
among carrots and apples
the piles of laundry on the washer
and the family sits in the flat light
as families do after company departs
and reweaves itself
over the gaps torn
by the abrupt arrivals and departures
the presence of strangers
so that in a month – days even –
husband or children pausing
over some familiar occupation
will mention a name
vaguely almost questioning
over their shoulders
and she will clench herself
around the names the shapes
forced down again until
they fester burst
within her

In the rear-view mirror
her face in series first
her hair curling again
complacently around her
forehead where wrinkles
erase themselves
and her eyes seem
to reflect the window light
like bits of glass
only the mouth refuses
its former thin-stitch
expands over the edges
of the mirror as she tilts
her head sounds fly
up from her throat

and in the blurred moment
of their rising she sees
herself again grow
multiple and magic lantern
shimmering
the windfrozen people on the street
emerging from the December light
figures in a stereoscope
a moment like the one
when you realize that magic
is not the trick itself
but the magician's hardworked skill
with coins and handkerchiefs
the complex possibilities
of common things

then silence
the rough weight of her duffel-coat
the cold circle of the steering-wheel
and the bare patches of pavement
as she drives slowly home
through the first snow
of the year

A STUBBORN GRACE

I

"The body chooses its own death" you told me once
and what I saw was the two of us
gathering purple hepaticas in a spring wood
or pulling carrots   dark earth
staining our hands   something that lyrical
that easy

neither of us knowing
what you meant
till now   your words taking root
in this room   in your eyes
that draw me
to your bedside and your warm hands
growing into mine

hands I have watched so often   stubborn
grace of them lifting a child or reaching
for food at your crowded table
shaping the pots you made   and miming
that crazy house you lived in on the coast

stubborn grace of them now   insistent
fingers trembling with the effort
to wipe your own face   administer
the medicines that keep your mind
above the pain like a swimmer
swimming alone in a steady current

the body chooses
and your hands attend the choice
while we who are helpless in the face of it
wince from your swollen abdomen your bedsores
bruises on your arms that won't heal now

it's you who demand music
and pretty nightgowns   visits from your friends
dividing your days among us
like the rings and necklaces you press
into our unwilling hands

it's not that you wanted to die
death wasn't some exotic fruit you stretched toward
it's not that kind of choosing that you talked of then
unable to explain what you meant
how could you

your body chooses its own death
and the meaning of it opens slowly
from within like any change
stubborn as your hands   their bones
like the bones of the earth
when they thrust the snow aside
with the coming of a different season

II

I always thought dying made a clean
sweep of it   imagined you high
and white on a narrow bed
scent of roses   organ music in the air
but here you are
in this tumult of orange-peels water
jugs   children's paintings   flowers
books and cans of ginger-ale

I always thought dying was crisp
and abrupt as the telegram   the late-night
phone-call   I thought they had a special place
for it to happen in   remote and antiseptic
but here where you are people come and go
with presents and news and unfinished business

the room fills up with whatever they bring
like the gifts the ancients placed
in the tombs of the dead
believing they carried the things
they loved in life
into the new land

a little like that and not
like that at all   as long as you're alive
the gifts we bring are used and put aside
the business stays unfinished   we can only give you
what's at hand for now   whatever we were doing
just before we came   you do the same
for us   and your dying weaves
through the muddle of our day
a single thread
in the cloth of another colour

I always thought death
was something you came up
against and entered
with deliberate ceremonies   formal words
but here where you are my own dying
enters me
like the song a friend might sing
in the last moments of a party
washing quietly through laughter   whispered
conversations   gradually gathering us up
until the last notes drop
into the still pools
the song has made in each of us
rippling through us as we reach
for our coats   murmur "thank you" and "goodbye"
drift out onto the street

III

In your house everyone is hungry
each morning your children's eager fingers
tear into the day   they eat
the heart out of it   cramming their mouths
with sunshine   nothing can stop
the noise   your mother clatters pots
in the kitchen and the house is stuffed
with food   we heap our plates
as if this sadness were an empty
stomach we could satisfy
like Christmas every day

there are salads crisp
and singing in their wooden bowls
two kinds of pie whipped cream and coffee
the talk is of holidays and summer
we grow fat on it   sated
with ocean beaches trips to the mountains

when I sit by your bed these nights
and you mutter   dreaming   half delirious
I am as greedy for your words as the woman
who wakes to her lover talking in his sleep
hovers above him jealous
of the conversation he is sharing somewhere else
I want you here again
and lean toward you calling
but your name is just another word
you've put aside for the ones
you are learning in the country of your dying

your mother stands at the doorway
folding her arms across her breasts
she cradles the absence of the child
she can't protect

and sometimes these nights it seems as if you are
a child again   a child sent on an errand alone
for the first time so eager
in her need to prove herself
beyond the anxious borders of her parents' care
that nothing can harm her

these nights in this house
where everyone is hungry   you are moving
far beyond our help with that same
eagerness   the boldness   the tenacious
beauty of it all the benediction
that you need   and when I leave you
for the night outside I am hungry
enough to eat the moon   make snowballs
with my bare hands and toss them at it
bite of them in my palms
as pieces of moonlight start
falling around me
in a bright rain

IV

and sometimes words are not
enough   they don't even matter

now you are dead and my grief
becomes a place I feel
I've lived in always
looking out at a world
where people come and go
with confident expressions on their faces
as if their plans for the day were solid
as the streets they walk on   secure
as the houses they return to every night

I look out at this other world
and the names of the objects in it
their uses fall away from me
like the names and faces of the people
who stand outside my borders now
saying "sorry" "sorry"

in these last few weeks your hands
grew whiter than the snow on your windowsill
and beside them mine
even in their pasty winter paleness
blushed   I was almost ashamed to touch you
I was so alive

but in the end it was our hands
that mattered   obdurate fact
of them   their colour   like the last
word between us
that and the touch
yours gave before it was withdrawn
leaving mine still curved

all any of us have perhaps

the shapes a hand makes
when words are no longer enough
and the depth of what can't be said
reaches
to the bone

Common Magic

THE TOWN WHERE I GREW UP

In the town where I grew up,
most of the people had ancestors
who were UELs and they still
liked things tidy, kept their yards
fenced and their noses clean.
After that, the things that mattered
most were last names
and being Protestant.

North of the town, the road
disintegrated into potholes and the dust
that weathered the grey shacks
where the grimy laundry flapping
in the trees was the flag
of another country.

Up there
people shooed the chickens
off the table when the pastor came.

Things happened.

Crops withered overnight, ramshackle
barns hid two-headed cattle and young
girls bore their fathers' children.

What went on up there
was a story in a foreign language.

Pieces of it drifted into town,
like scraps of paper, catching
on the neat white fences
in the shaded streets.

Them and us.

I used to believe this.
Used to imagine an invisible
border, like the Maginot Line
we learned about in school,
between the teeming farms
that bordered our town
and the bare-boned fields beyond
where the shacks grew.

Now I think it's merely
a matter of emphasis,
like the *Globe & Mail*
and the *National Enquirer*.
They're both the same, really;
they both line words
like bars across the pages,
making you want to squeeze
between them into the white
where you think the truth is.

Each spring the countryside
fills up with lilacs. Every house
in town, every farm, every shack
has a clump of white or purple
at the doorstep. And on the road north,
bushes occur in the fields, alone,
not a house in sight for miles.
You might think they'd grown wild,
but you'd be wrong. Planted for good luck
by the early settlers, the lilacs continue
long after the farms fail and houses
weather away.

Flags of a different kind.

They indicate the subterranean counties
plotted underneath the sleekest pastures,
the sanest red-brick houses.
And rooted in the littered dark,
as dreams are, they bloom
each May as if they were
the only living things on earth.

LONELY FOR THE COUNTRY

Sometimes these days
you think you are ready
to settle down.

This might be the season for it,
this summer of purple sunsets
when you stand in the streets
watching the sky, until its colour
is a bruised place
inside your chest.

When you think of settling down
you imagine yourself growing comfortable
with the land and remember the sunstained faces
of men like your grandfather, the ridges of black veins
that furrowed the backs of their hands as they squared
a county boundary for you, or built once more
old Stu McKenzie's barn exactly as they'd raised it
60 years ago.
You watch the hands of the women
on market days, piling onions, filling buckets
with tomatoes, their thick, workaday gestures
disclosing at times
what you think you recognize as caring,
even love.

At least that's how it looks
from the outside and when you think
of settling down, you always think of it
as a place.

It makes the city seem imaginary, somehow.
As you drive through the streets,
you begin to see how the lives there look
as if they had been cut from magazines:
a blond couple carrying a wicker picnic-basket

through the park, a man in faded brown shorts
squatting on his front lawn
fixing a child's red bike.

You wish you could tell yourself
that this is all too sentimental.
You want to agree with the person
who said, "There's no salvation
in geography."

But you can't
and you're beginning to suspect
that deep within you,
like a latent gene, is this belief
that we belong somewhere.

What you know
is that once you admit that
it opens in you
a deeper need.
A need like that loneliness
which makes us return again and again
to the places we've shared
with those we can no longer love,
empty-hearted, yet expectant,
searching for revelations
in the blank faces of remembered houses.

As wide as bereavement
and dangerous,
it renders us innocent
as mourners at a graveside
who want to believe their loss
has made this holy ground
and wait
for the earth beneath their feet
to console them.

PLACE OF ORIGIN

One by one my friends move away
to become legends. What news I have of them
arrives like postcards with foreign stamps
or those messages that always look
as if the person who wrote them
was thinking of something else the whole time.

Me, I keep on living here, without meaning to.
Friends ask me why, I say *light*,
I say *lake*, I say *cost of housing*,
but it doesn't add up and most of them know it.
The ones who don't tell me how nice it must be
to feel rooted. Like an oak tree
or as if my feeling for the place
were something I could cultivate
as easily as turnips or potatoes.
Other people take me to the mountains,
or try to make me love an ocean,
but all I can see are more postcards.
"Too fancy for me," I tell them,
trying to keep it casual,
but my face muscles start to rearrange themselves:
my grandfather's look, half-sullen, half-sly
whenever anyone would mention Toronto or Montreal.
The look that told you most people were tourists to him
and there was nothing he could do about it.
(Meaning, he didn't want to.
Meaning, he'd never been twenty miles from his hometown
and that was enough for him.)

For most places, there are two kinds of geography
and it's no different here.
The men know land and weather,
who owns it and for how long,
what to prepare for when you can.

Being men, they have access to maps
and county records, almanacs.
Their wives know it differently.
Not just who married who
but what it was like and why,
how the kids turned out in the end.
This may be gossip,
but that doesn't make it unimportant.
You can't have your daughters marrying men
who beat their wives, raising children
who will tear all over the countryside
making fools of themselves.
"What's bred in the bone," my grandmother said,
"comes out in the flesh."

All of which I can accept, like the look
in my mother's eyes these days
when she tells me of another wedding or another death,
saying it's time for you to learn all this.
(Meaning, some day you have to decide
what you're doing here.)
But I'm not sure I want it.
I could tell you that this place
holds me like a family and mean it,
but that also means it holds me back.
These people who know who I am, who I've been, for generations
assume a certain ownership
and the hard part is, I recognize their right.

I wanted something simpler,
a place of origin,
direct as the love I imagined feeling for the dead,
believing grief made love perfect.
But even the dead go on changing,
whether I want to admit it or not,
there's always another coming to terms
and another.

My friends keep on asking
what I'm doing here and I keep on
not having the answer.
The thing I worry about most though
is that my children are getting older
and I could get stuck here
through another generation, without meaning to.
The thing I keep seeing is my grandfather's face,
letting you know that Toronto and Montreal
were nothing to him, he belonged right here.
Bluffing you
into believing it.

DISTANCE FROM HARROWSMITH TO TAMWORTH

Beside me, Jeremy is searching for the North West Territories,
white with red letters in the shape of a polar bear.
It's all he needs to complete Canada,
though he won't find it here on 38,
only a few tourists heading north to cottage country,
the rest, local traffic,
people who've no place else to go but home.

The farm where my father was born
is on the left, a mile outside of Harrowsmith,
my grandfather too, and my great-grandfather.
Now my cousin's there with his new wife
and already the old barns square their shoulders,
the silos straighten, eager for the birth of a son,
they seem to crowd the house, as if there's still not room enough
to separate love from geography.

Like the back of my hand, we say
for the place we come to call home,
the claim we can only make
through the hands, planting food and children.

Even my two gripping the steering-wheel
know this road as a hunger I can't help
giving in to: "Look," I say to Jeremy
as we pull into Hartington, "there's the school
where your grandmother taught before she met Grandpa,"
baiting him, hoping he'll bite for the rest of the story,
though I'll tell it anyway. His grandmother, from Enterprise,
just happening to get that school, just happening
to board at the farm across the way,
which belonged to some uncle or other of his grandfather's
who was helping out there for a bit,
as if he were meant to meet her, I want to say, make him hear
the story the way I did – how he was slopping pigs that first day

when she came up the lane, so that she thought he was the
hired man
and said that at dinner, everyone laughing at her –
how it seemed to me then that the distance between
Enterprise and Hartington was immense, impossible, amazing
to discover that out of all those back roads and misunderstandings
and incomprehensible adult laughter should come my mother
and my father.

I'm still trying to explain it when we turn west at Verona,
but I've hardly finished a sentence before
we're at Bellrock, where my father's mother was born
and moved from, to another farm on 38, just in time
to meet my grandfather, and after Bellrock,
Enterprise, the very house my mother lived in as a girl,
twenty minutes from Hartington, at the most,
but, oh Jeremy, so much farther really.
Listen, I try to say, *listen!*
This is the most important story
you will ever hear.
Except that it isn't
and Jeremy leans forward, playing with the radio.
He has his own magic parent, after all;
his father lives 400 miles away,
arrives on a black Yamaha for technicolour weekends;
even the long times in between are filled
with the tapes they send instead of letters
once a week, Jeremy alone in his room
talking to a machine and able to make it sound
like an ordinary conversation.
Who am I to say what distances he should believe in,
these towns rush together, like my words or the fields
he swims through, so much green noise.

In the ditches *Purple Loosestrife, Horseweed,*
Fleabane, St John's Wort, names I learned only this year
to make the flowers more familiar. Like these stories,

all I have to call a country,
rich as blood, placenta for my future
already seeded in the fields or that woman's face
in the last town, the curve of the road there
as it turns toward the next, *Tamworth* people say
for this one, needing something
to make it sound like a choice,
whatever holds them here,
whatever they've come to love enough.

MY SON IS LEARNING TO INVENT

My son is learning to invent
himself. Today he tells me of a time
I took him to a hospital and left him
alone there. He describes how he shook the steel
bars of his crib and cried as I left the room
without looking back.

(He was three. He had pneumonia
and I was alone. For a week,
I slept in a chair by his bed.
I only left once to buy him a book
when he was asleep.
The child in the next bed
had tubes in her throat and no-one
came to visit her at all.)

My son holds up his hands. If he could,
he would show me the desperate
welts the crib bars left and the black
square of my back cutting the light
from his eyes.

But I shake my head.

Stalemate.

Sometimes I show him pictures of myself
when I was his age. There is one
where I sit with my kid brother
in the middle of my grandfather's garden.
This is the one my son likes best.
But he insists that the boy,
my brother, who is fat and freckled,
is himself.

"Don't be ridiculous," I tell him,
"that's your Uncle Cam."

He tosses the photograph aside
and refuses to lose himself
in family history. What good is it
to him? Like that stupid riddle
about the sound of a tree falling
alone in a forest of trees.
The sun that shines over
these other children's heads
might as well be shining over
an empty pasture for all he cares.

In the top right corner of the photograph
is the cornfield where the children played
hide-and-go-seek.
We are still there, of course,
only now it is my son and I
who stalk each other
through the thin, green
leaves that bristle our bare arms
and whisper as they fold behind us, dry
secrets only they understand.

Whose childhood is this, anyway?

When we play in the park, he rides
in a swing so high above my head
the peak of his cap is a dark arrow
aimed at the heart of the sun.

"Look!" he calls.

And he lets go.

Only his body sinks through the abrupt
air toward concrete and the horrible
sound my throat can't make.

When the rest of the park
begins to move again
he is sprawled on his stomach
in the grass beyond the swing.

He gets to his feet
and his face is the colour of milk,
his lips sucked in
like an old man's.

I open my mouth, as he looks
up at me, wiping his palms on his jeans.
"Were you scared?" he asks.

My son is learning.

INTO THE MIDST OF IT

You'll take a map, of course, and keep it
open in front of you on the dashboard,
though it won't help. Oh, it'll give mileages,
boundary lines, names, that sort of thing,
but there are places yet
where names are powerless
and what you are entering
is like the silence words get lost in
after they've been spoken.

It's the same with the highways.
The terse, comforting numbers
and the signs that anyone can read.
They won't be any good to you now.
And it's not that kind of confidence
you're after anyway.

What you're looking for are the narrower,
unpaved roads that have become
the country they travel over, dreamlike
as the spare farms you catch
in the corner of your eye,
only to lose them
when you turn your head. The curves
that happen without warning
like a change of heart,
as if, after all these journeys,
the road were still feeling
its way through.

A man comes up on your right – blue shirt
patched from the sky – solid and
unsurprised. He doesn't turn his head
at your passing and by the time your eyes move
to the rear-view mirror, the road has changed.

But it's then you begin to notice
other people: women hanging clothes from grey
porches, a clutter of children on the steps.
Like the man, they do not move
as you go by and you try to imagine
how you must look to them: metallic glimmer
on the bright rim of their sky,
disturbing the dust
that settles behind you, slowly,
through the day's heat,
while in your mind's eye, their faces
form and change with the rippling patterns
sun and cloud make on the fields,
like the figures that swim below your thoughts
in the hour between dream and waking.

It makes you think of the people you love,
how their faces look when they don't know you're watching them,
so that what you see there
forces you to recognize
how useless your love is, how little
all your hopes, your good intentions
can ever do for them.

Only now, this doesn't hurt any more,
becomes part of your love, in a way,
just as the dry-weather drone of the cicada
belongs to the heat, to the dust that sifts
like ash over the shiny leaves,
this country you're travelling through,
where the farmlands draw their nourishment
from an ancient mountain range,
and houses rise, insistent
as the rock and almost as indifferent,
making all your questions
about why people came here,
what they liked about it,

why they stayed
as meaningless as questions you might ask
of the trees or the earth itself.

You, who have lived your whole life believing
if you made enough plans
you wouldn't need to be afraid,
driving through a countryside
only the road seems to care about,
to rediscover every time it enters
with that kind of love that's partly tenderness
and partly a sort of confidence
you can't put words around.
Like the look
the people at home will give you
when you get there: nonchalant and almost too deep
for you to see, as they turn back
to whatever held them
before you came.

MEXICAN SUNSETS

Somewhere in Mexico, a volcano erupts,
spewing dust that drifts northward
disturbing the atmosphere of Southern Ontario
so that all this autumn, small, grey
English-speaking towns are startled
by inordinate sunsets: shameless
fuchsias, brazen corals flaunt
their outlandish origins in a country
where anything can happen.

Nothing's the same any more.
Here in Kingston, even limestone forgets itself
and the staid Protestant church towers
succumb to gothic fantasies, windows ablaze
with dragons' fire and the pink screams
of captured damsels; while the bare, old
branches of trees are elegant filigrees,
burnt black and delicate
by so much colour.

It's November, but no-one believes it.
Winter's a crass rumour like the threat
of a layoff or a government's economic policy.
And the people inhabiting the lavender streets
have the stature of fabled creatures
from that land we all believe in, somewhere
between imagination and nostalgia.

You could call it
a state of grace, although
it's only for a season, like the love
we risk for each other
on the first fine day in March,
or during the perfect anarchy
of a heavy snowfall

when everyone's late for work
and doesn't give a damn.

A kind of conspiracy
we let ourselves get caught in,
half-bewildered, half-encouraged
by the sky's extravagance, this
fragile crust of earth
pulsing beneath us.

COMMON MAGIC

Your best friend falls in love
and her brain turns to water.
You can watch her lips move,
making the customary sounds,
but you can see they're merely
words, flimsy as bubbles rising
from some golden sea where she
swims sleek and exotic as a mermaid.

It's always like that.
You stop for lunch in a crowded
restaurant and the waitress floats
toward you. You can tell she doesn't care
whether you have the baked or french-fried
and you wonder if your voice comes
in bubbles too.

It's not just women either. Or love
for that matter. The old man
across from you on the bus holds
a young child on his knee; he is singing
to her and his voice is a small boy
turning somersaults in the green
country of his blood.
It's only when the driver calls his stop
that he emerges into this puzzle
of brick and tiny hedges. Only then
you notice his shaking hands, his need
of the child to guide him home.

All over the city
you move in your own seasons
through the seasons of others: old women, faces
clawed by weather you can't feel
clack dry tongues at passersby

while adolescents seethe
in their glassy atmospheres of anger.

In parks, the children
are alien life-forms, rooted
in the galaxies they've grown through
to get here. Their games weave
the interface and their laughter
tickles that part of your brain where smells
are hidden and the nuzzling textures of things.

It's a wonder that anything gets done
at all: a mechanic flails
at the muffler of your car
through whatever storm he's trapped inside
and the mailman stares at numbers
from the haze of a distant summer.
Yet somehow letters arrive and buses
remember their routes. Banks balance.
Mangoes ripen on the supermarket shelves.
Everyone manages. You gulp the thin air
of this planet as if it were the only
one you knew. Even the earth you're
standing on seems solid enough.
It's always the chance word, unthinking
gesture that unlocks the face before you.
Reveals the intricate countries
deep within the eyes. The hidden
lives, like sudden miracles,
that breathe there.

CHARLIE'S YARD

Some things have an order
that isn't planned. In Charlie's yard
the woodpile leans toward the necessary
laws of gravity enough to keep it
upright, but its true symmetry comes
more from anger: clean bite of it
and axe in Charlie's hands,
driving deep into the sullen heart
of a solitary night. After his wife left
the only things that Charlie brought
from the farm they'd shared
were bits of machinery, scraps he liked
the shapes and colours of. They rust in the green
of his garden, plough discs and wagon wheels.
Each one has its place somehow, an authority
tranquil as an old man's, who has worked
all his life with his hands, until even his mind
moves around thoughts with the same
unhurried grace. It's like that wicker chair
abandoned in the middle of the yard. No-one intended
to leave it there, just drifted off toward
whatever plans they'd made while sitting in it.
Now, it's rooted there as surely
as the tree behind it, weathered into place
like the bare grey boards of the tool-shed.
Some things have an order
that isn't planned. They seem aimless
as the hours a man spends waiting
for the woman he loves,
a pot of coffee going muddy on the stove.
It's just when he's given up
he turns to find her, framed by the white
wood of his doorway and the blue sky
caught in her hair.

COMING THROUGH

It's the time of day you like best: that hour
just before dark, when the colours
and shapes of things seem to forget
their daylit boundaries, so that the sound
of someone whistling in the street is the last pink
light on the horizon, fading through other sounds
of traffic and laughter into lilac, into blue-grey.

Nothing is solid now. Against the sky the trees
are so still they vibrate with the effort
of holding themselves in and the walls of the houses
hesitate as if they might dissolve,
revealing the lives behind them, intricate
and enchanted as the lives of dolls.

You had a friend who opened
secrets for you like that
and when you think of her now
it's mostly on evenings like this one,
when the last of that light
which is itself a kind of silence
gives to the room a mirror-like quality,
translucent as a memory.

You can almost smell the coffee you'd make for her then,
see the steam rising from the blue cup, her fingers
curled around it, warming themselves.
You can still see the way her hands moved
when she talked, creating a second language,
drawing you in
to the very centre of her words
where the real stories lived.

And her eyes, following your sentences
wherever they led,
until it seemed those nights
you entered each other's lives
as if they were countries,
not the superficial ones that maps create,
or ordinary conversation, but the kind
that twist and plummet underneath a day's events
like the labyrinths you followed as a child
or the new-made world that opened
for you alone when you discovered lying.

You lived within each other then
and each of those nights was a place
you inhabited together, a place
you thought you could return to always.

The headlights from a passing car outside
startle the bright ghosts that gather
in the corners of the room. It makes you remember
the bedroom you had as a child
and how you huddled under the covers like a snail,
watching the goblins who lived in the dresser drawers
glide across the mirror and over the ceiling
into your bed. It was the smell of your teddy bear
that saved you then and the satin edge of the blanket
at your cheek as smooth as sleep.
It was the voices of your parents in the kitchen,
far away as growing up and as safe. Even by day
your parents filled their lives with such a confidence,
you believed they had been born into adulthood
or arrived there, years ago, before
there were any history-books or maps, and made it
their very own sort of place. Not like you.

Stubbing your toes on the furniture that changed
overnight, your arms suddenly appearing
from the sleeves of your favourite jacket
like a scarecrow's,
like somebody else.
You can laugh at it now, although
it's only lately you've begun to realize
how much of your time you've spent like that:
almost a guest in your own life,
wandering around waiting for someone
or something to explain things to you.

It was always late when she left
and you'd stand in the doorway, waiting
till she'd started the car, then
sit in the dark yourself
for the twenty minutes or so it took her
to drive home. As you locked up, checked the kids
you could imagine her doing the same thing,
so that on those nights sleep was just another opening,
another entry you made together.

She's been dead for a long time now.
You'd thought that would make a difference,
but it hasn't. And though you feel angry
at your need for an explanation
it's still there. As if she owed it to you somehow.
As if somebody did.

Oh, you've learned the accepted wisdom of it.
Can even feel yourself healing these days, almost
strong enough now to re-enter the place
you inhabited together. And you know
you'll never figure it all out anyway;
any more than you can understand your neighbours
from what you see in their lighted windows
framed, like public advertisements.
And yet.

A part of you resists all that.
Resists it with the pure, unthinking stubbornness
you lived in as a child,
that harder wisdom
you are rediscovering now.
Some people are a country
and their deaths displace you.
Everything you shared with them
reminds you of it: part of you in exile
for the rest of your life.

DAILY NEWS

There are days when I try to imagine the planet
pausing once in a while, like an old woman
on the edge of her bed, who sounds her bones
for the reaches her dying has made
while she slept.

These are the times when I believe
that old men do remember keener weather,
that January when their words froze in the air
or an August so blank with heat
that all it left was the smell
of the crops drying in the fields.
"It's all out of kilter now," one of them tells me,
"just more of the same all year round,"
and I want to believe the planet feels this
as a falling away she wants to tell us about
before it's too late.

Last week, a 20,000-year-old mastodon tusk
was washed up on Virginia Beach.
I believe we should take this
as a direct warning, or better still
a cry for help.

What I want most to believe, though,
is that we're all in this together.

As it is, I hardly know what to look for.
The birthrate's rising slightly, but
according to a recent survey
most teenagers can't see the point
of planning for the future.
Even my friends don't seem to feel
that what they're living these days
is a real life.

Instead, I hear men telling me
that victory is a nuclear war
which 60 million people survive.
I think they really believe this
and what's more, I'm sure it's nothing
to what they can do
whenever they want.

This is the point where I realize
how arrogant it is
to imagine the planet caring about all this.
Though I admit to the image
of a bitter woman longing for a death
that takes her whole family with her,
the mastodon tusk should be enough
to let us know
we're only another species after all.
Meanwhile, my son says he gets scared sometimes
on the way home from school
that they'll drop the bomb
before he makes it.
The worst part though
is how his voice is
when he tells me this.
How he doesn't ask
what he can do about it.

Meanwhile, I read in the papers
that they found a skeleton
that proves whales used to live on land.
And on another page, how doctors managed
to replace a man's left hand with his right
after both were cut off in an accident.
It's going to be okay too, although
"it looks very strange," the man reports.
"Suddenly I'm looking at a hand with fingers.
A hand. It's like getting married
to someone you don't know."

REMINDER

In a crowded theatre lobby, the perfume
in a strange woman's hair nudges a jealousy
I thought I'd put down years ago.
Unlocks that stubborn convolution of my brain
where it rears and spits.
Even my fingers turn to claws.

Smells like fists.
One whiff of feta cheese and olives
numbs my solar plexus with the blow of a first love,
while freesias are a falling into something deeper,
a loss I haven't even named yet.

I'm told that smell is centred
in our first brain. Primitive,
lizard part of us still cautiously sniffing
its way through colours and mysteries.
The world as it is before we discover
how to shape it into names,
learn to use language like a hope
for the future. Something that could save us
if we use it carefully, put enough words
between ourselves and the past.

A man and a woman sit in an all-night
restaurant. She's smoking cigarettes,
he's drinking cup after cup
of black coffee, double sugar.
They're in one of those conversations
you don't need words to follow,
though they're using enough of them, their mouths
so rigid with choosing that the lips
have thinned to that whiteness you find
outside pain, if you tighten your muscles hard enough.

And maybe it's only because I can't hear
what they're saying that I imagine
this other sound, somewhere between a feeling
and a voice. An ache in the bone that sings
of an old wound. Something you can't put
your finger on. Right now, it's cautionary,
like a growl, though already their bodies
cringe at it and their hands ride
the waves of its swelling.

Sooner or later it will
rise and she'll start screaming;
he'll retreat into that baffled
silence men sometimes use for tears.

This isn't a lesson in body-language.
It's more like a warning, though there's not
much we can do. We can't go back
to nuzzling and grunting at each other,
trying to sniff out anger or love.
And there's no such thing
as a simpler time anyway.

You might call it
a reminder, like the dinosaur
bone in the museum,
the one we can touch,
the one worn smooth
with our need.

Meanwhile, the man and woman go on
talking and I can imagine how their mouths
must ache for a word that's as explicit
as the click of her lighter,
his definitive way of measuring
the two teaspoonsful of sugar.
Words are their hope for the future.

They've cherished them like children.
And now their faces have the puzzled,
fragile look of parents
who have taken great care
and are always surprised
to see the past they thought
they'd freed their children from
assert itself. In their way of walking,
in their laughter,
in their sullen, indifferent eyes.

WOMAN AT THE NEXT

The woman at the next table is angry.
Angry in that dogged, repetitive way
a woman gets when she's had a few drinks.
Not enough to make her inarticulate,
but enough so that her voice has become something
you can feel, like the beginning of a headache,
at your temples or the back of your neck.

She's talking about men
and you've heard it all before:
in restaurants and elevators, at parties,
on a flight to Vancouver once, for five hours
the woman behind you going on and on.
Even the people she's with have stopped
trying to answer and are working hard
at being quiet and small.
Like children enduring a scolding
they look as if her voice has shoved them
into their seats and is holding them there.
Which it is, of course,
so that as you watch them, words and hands
get muddled in your mind
until they seem like the same thing.

Sometimes a person's hands
are the only words he knows.
A fat man sitting in a hospital waiting-room
after they have taken his wife
or his child away from him
bows his head beneath the doctor's level voice
and sees how the high, white vowels
of his clenched fists
begin in the darker sound
his heart is making.

Sometimes a man's words
are the holes he makes with these fists
in the brittle whine of his wife's complaint.
Everyone knows what a woman's scorn
is supposed to be like,
how we can eat a man with laughter
over a cup of coffee.

Which doesn't say much
for the woman at the next table.
Drunker now, her voice has gone teary and pale.
The only thing she'll want to eat tomorrow
are her own words.

That's what the people around her
are counting on: tomorrow
when she'll be right back
where she started, waiting on tables somewhere
or cleaning someone's house,
getting home late and ironing the kids' clothes
while she watches TV.
You can tell by her hands
that she works hard,
words are what she really binges on,
like someone cheating on a diet,
putting some more fat
between herself and her pain.

What gets you, of course,
is that you recognize the tendency
though you hate to admit it.
Hate to think of all the nights
you've spent like that,
all the mornings
waking from this dream
of your own voice
to the fumbling memory,
dead weight on the day.

"Getting it off your chest," it's called
though you can see now
that it doesn't make any sense
pretending anger is something you catch
like a bad cold
and then throw off again
in a couple of weeks.

You used to believe there was too much
anger in the world.
Now you think maybe there isn't enough.
Not the kind you can use anyway.
The kind that strips things down
to the cleaned, bare bones, naked and efficient,
shaped to fit the hand like a weapon.

Maybe it's like that somewhere else,
but you suspect
a lot of nights are just like this one;
anger slurred to tears
tomorrow's hangover already coating the tongue.
The kind of night that sends you into the streets
half-hoping for an accident or a fire,
the sound of sirens slicing into it
stopping everything cold.

HOW IT WILL HAPPEN

In this town
it's times like these
make a woman realize exactly
how her job is going to destroy her.

It won't be an accident either.
The sudden sheering of metal or rock
that gets you in a factory, a mine.
Even now, the woman can feel it coming on
like one of those slow diseases
of the joint or the bone
that doctors diagnose in terms you recognize
as bigger words for dying.

Her job is to sit at a desk all day,
talking to people who come at her
through a smudged glass door
that gets kicked in every week or so
by someone who didn't get what they wanted
or someone else who realized suddenly
that they never would.

After eight hours
she can go home.
Which is the problem.
Which is what makes her think
that maybe they're right,
the people who say a woman gets too personal
in a job like this, a problem of hormones maybe,
something in the size of the breasts,
the position of the uterus.

She envies younger girls.
The way they snap their desk drawers shut
at 4:30 sharp, snap open their makeup cases,
paint their lips bright red.

Their laughter comes
from a great distance,
the way she imagines it must sound
to the woman she saw at 3:45.
The woman whose husband hit her so hard
he broke her middle ear,
sending the sounds of her own screams back
in a roar of blood.

Women and children.
In a town like this
where there aren't enough factories
to keep them busy, the women
take welfare. Their kids
take to the streets, surviving
on small stuff
until something comes along
that's big enough
to put them in jail for a few years.
The woman sees eight or ten a day.
Boys mostly. About her son's age.
Usually they stare at the floor
while she talks to them, arms folded
over their chests. And even when they do
look her in the eye
all she can see any more
are the faces they've learned to wear
for high-school principals, truant officers,
youth workers, cops.

Reminds her of that game she used to play
at the cottage, in August, when there was nothing
left to do: hauling waterlogged wood
out of the bay, to push it
over the edge of the dock,
watch it sink again
into the thick, dull water.

Since this is a prison town
most of the guys you read about
on the front pages
are here somewhere.
So are their wives and kids,
like camp-followers,
waiting for the next move.
Lots of times though
the next move takes so long
that by the time the guy gets out
even on a day-pass,
the families have disappeared.
These are the ones the woman feels most sorry for;
so she takes them out to a show
or invites them home for dinner.

At Christmas it was Tyler.
His first day out in ten years.
The woman remembers two things:
the hours he spent just sitting in her kitchen
studying the pattern pale sun made
with the plants in the window and the smoke
from his cigarettes;
and the way he stared
at her daughter's breasts
when she poured him coffee.
At night when she lies down
a voice drones in her head, like one of those tapes
you can play by your pillow
to help you learn things while you sleep.

It's only a job, the voice tells her,
only a job. And there's only
so much you can do
for people like that.
They have to learn
to help themselves.
But each day still
heaves itself in, white and graceless.
The same faces set themselves against her
and her words stumble in a need
that has nothing to do with help at all.

In a town like this,
it's times like these
make a woman see more clearly
how it will happen.
It isn't a matter of keeping on
or quitting. Nothing as clear as that.
But the look
on her son's face when he says
he wants to be a cop or a prison guard
(though he's only fourteen and you can't tell
with boys his age) because he's sick
of all this wishy-washy bleeding
heart crap. Wants to be a cop
so he can have things cut and dried.

It's watching him say that,
knowing he means it.
Knowing she wants the same thing herself.
Only differently.

DREAMS OF RESCUE

In the dream
the car is a sound,
a screech of brakes that tears a hole
in the sunlight, big enough
for the dog to flop through,
fish-like guts spilling on the side of the road.

In the dream
the children's voices
crying *do something do something*
are a mist I grope through, fingers thick
as my tongue with the smell of dust and blood.

A telephone grows from my hand
and my cry for help recedes into the churn
and whining of machinery
that rings
and rings
and rings
me into 3-AM darkness, cold
floor under my feet
and your voice
coming at me from the coast.

"*Pour yourself a drink,*" you say,
"*I'm paying.*"

It's only midnight where you are
two hours into a bottle and your second
pack of cigarettes, but there's no use arguing
and somehow the scotch I pour
cuts through time-zones and Prairie winters
until night and distance
are another room in this house
we are learning to build: two women

sitting up late, sharing out our days
with the whisky and the cigarettes.

Something has happened to you.
In your voice it's a kind of tenderness
that hovers over your words – like a mother
watching her kid learn to walk –
as if you could protect them
from what they must say.

You're telling me what you're reading
these days, titles I recognize, names.
Each one flares for a moment, struck match
that pulls some reassuring object
– watch-face, ashtray, scotch bottle –
out of the darkness
where your face bobs, white and scared.
Little sister.
When you were three
you were a pain in the ass.
All that summer at the cottage
watching you, waiting for you
and then that one morning for one moment
turning my back and turning again
to find you face down in the water.

I wouldn't call it love that pulled you
up by the arm and thumped you on the back
so hard your head snapped,
shook you till your face streamed snot
and tears, till you screamed, till you promised
never to tell, till I couldn't see you for the sun
and the sound of my own crying, fist
in the guts that taught me for the first time
how words like that are just a clumsy warning
scrawled at the border of a terrifying country.

Little sister:
most of the time you were just that.
A royal pain in the ass.
When I left for college
you were still playing dress-up;
it's only lately we've become
like any women,
starting from scraps of the past
and the rest of our lives
trying to find words that fit.

This pause that stretches between us now
is a tightrope, taut wire alive with waiting,
click of your lighter
catch in your breath
as you exhale smoke
begin:

"We're splitting, Carl and I."

"A lot of things. He   he tried
to beat me up, hit me with his fists
at first, we got a marriage counsellor
but

(First, he hit you with his fists.
First, he hit you.)

"but then he   he came at me
with a hammer   tore my shoulder
broke my nose …

"I've been in one of those houses
you know   for battered women …
"Pretty good   met some women here
it's all right   I'm okay
now   I …

Your voice trails away from me
into the lie you couldn't possibly finish
and like the cramped limb that wakes
the sleeper from a nightmare, stab of pain
in my palm, white grip of it
on the telephone receiver, pulls me up
into this room and if you were here, I swear
I could shake you till your head snapped.
Shake you the way a mother will shake a child
who has run beyond her into a scream
of brakes, as if she could shake her
into safety and herself free
of her own fierce helplessness.

You are crying now
and the sound reaches for me
through the distances
your husband's hands have forced
between us;
between what we must live
and what we can tell.

I think of all those proverbs
only a woman would use.
Our grandmother's cold comfort:

Marry in haste, repent at leisure.

You've made your bed. Now you must
lie in it.

Wisdom of women
whose only choice
was to choose someone else
and a lifetime at the halted limit
of that reaching.
All those dreams of rescue
we dreamed we'd put aside.

Your voice against all that.

Three thousand miles away
in a city I barely know
the man you love
has beaten you with a hammer
and if what needed to be said
were something a woman could make
from whatever she had on hand,
like a cut-down dress
like a good warm coat,
I would stay up all night
to finish it for you.

In the house that sheltered you
a woman's hands have rubbed your shoulders,
brought you tea and the names of lawyers,
the tides of books that might help.
And when you couldn't stand it,
when terror was a muffled weight
on your chest, thick as fur
over your mouth,
there was always a woman there
to hold you.

It means you'll survive all this
though we both know you'll never
get over it. There'll always be a need
for something tougher: a skin you could wrap
your heart in, fold it away
from this grieving that stuns you
with its news of a death.

"I only needed to hear your voice," you tell me.
"Just for a while. It's better now. Goodnight."

"Goodnight. Take care of yourself."

But sleep comes piecemeal,
teased by the goblin shapes
of what I could have, should have said.
I will be glad for morning,
for the brief light that delivers us
into its own kind of certainty
where the dream you woke me from
becomes a message I can puzzle over.
While the love I feel for you now
is like the story a mother tells her child
at bedtime, knowing it only serves
to carry her into a land of strangers
where she must dream her own rescue
from whatever scraps and fragments of it
she finds, wrecked there.

TO GET TO YOU

It's never easy.
Even the effort of a few steps
from the bedroom to the kitchen, say,
or a few muscles, opening my eyes
to find you still there in bed beside me
is an act of magic or faith,
I'm never sure which.

All I know is that it's learned
by doing, over and over again,
like any other trick,
until you don't need to think about it.
Like now. Like the way I'm walking home
to you through this city I've learned to accept
as the only kind there is: five o'clock,
night coming down and rain
just hard enough
to make the crowds on the corners shove a little
when a bus finally splashes to the stop.
Outside a restaurant, two men shake hands
and a little boy holds his father's
as they watch a toy airplane turning in a shop window.
It could be anywhere. But what I want you to notice
are the women. They are wearing white nurses' shoes,
or dirty sneakers or high-heeled boots.
They carry briefcases and flowers, bags of groceries
as they hurry home to their husbands and kids,
lovers, ailing parents, friends.
We all have the same look somehow.

See: over there by the bank
how that stout woman lowers her eyes
when she passes that group of boys,
how her movement's mimed
by the blonde, turning her head

when a car slows down beside her.
Even the high-pitched giggle of the girls
in that bunch of teenagers is a signal
I've learned to recognize. Tuned in
on my own tightened muscles, jawline or shoulders.
In fact, you might study the shoulders.
The line of the backbone too; arms and hips,
the body carried
like something the woman's not sure what to do with.

I've already told you that this is an ordinary city.
There are maps of it and lights to show us
when to walk, where to turn.
What I want you to know is that it isn't enough.

On a trip to Vancouver once
I discovered clearer landmarks. Red ones,
sprayed on sidewalks all over the city.
They marked the places
where a woman had been raped,
so that when I stepped out of a coffee shop
to find one on the pavement by the laundromat
geography shifted.
Brought me to the city I'd always imagined
happening in dark alleys, deserted parking-lots,
to somebody else. Brought me home in a way,
no longer the victim of rumours or old news,
that red mark planted in the pavement
like the flag of an ancient, immediate war.

I used to hope it was enough
that you are gentle,
that I love you,
but what can enough mean any more,
what can it measure?

How many rapes were enough
for those women in Vancouver
before they got stencils and spray paint
made a word for their rage?
How many more until even that word
lost its meaning
and the enemy was anything that moved out there.
Anything male, that is.

How can any woman say
she loves a man enough
when every city on the planet
is a minefield
she must pick her way through
just to reach him?

It's not that we manage it though.
It's that we make it look so easy.
These women wearing their fear
like a habit of speech or movement
as if this were the way
the female's body's meant to be.
The way I turn the last corner now,
open the door to find you
drinking wine and reading the newspaper,
another glass already filled
and waiting on the coffee-table.

When I turn on the hall light
the city will retreat into the rain,
the tiny squares of yellow
marking the other rooms
where men and women greet each other.
It's a matter of a few steps,
magic or faith, though it's not that simple.

The way the rain keeps watering the cities of the world.
How it throws itself against our window,
harder, more insistent,
so that we both hear.

THINKING WITH THE HEART

For Mary di Michele

I work from awkwardness. By that I mean I don't like to arrange things.
If I stand in front of something, instead of arranging it, I arrange myself
– Diane Arbus

The problem with you women is, you think with your hearts
– Policeman

How else to say it
except that the body is a limit
I must learn to love,
that thought is no different from flesh
or the blue pulse that rivers my hands.
How else, except to permit myself
this heart and its seasons,
like the cycles of the moon
which never seem to get me anywhere
but back again, not out.

Thought should be linear.
That's what the policeman means
when I bring the woman to him,
what he has to offer for her bruises, the cut
over her eye: *charge him or we can't help you.*
He's seen it all before anyway. He knows
how the law changes, depending on what you think.
It used to be a man could beat his wife
if he had to; now, sometimes he can't
but she has to charge him
and nine times out of ten
these women who come in here
ready to get the bastard
will be back in a week or so
wanting to drop the whole thing

because they're back together,
which just means a lot of paperwork
and running around for nothing.
It drives him crazy, how a woman
can't make up her mind and stick to it,
get the guy out once and for all.
"Charge him," he says, "or we won't help."

Out of her bed then, her house, her life,
but not her head, no, nor her children,
out from under her skin.
Not out of her heart, which goes on
in its slow, dark way, wanting
whatever it is hearts want
when they think like this;
a change in his, probably,
a way to hold what the heart can't
without breaking: how the man who beats her
is also the man she loves.
I wish I could show you
what a man's anger makes
of a woman's face,
or measure the days it takes
for her to emerge from a map of bruises
the colour of death. I wish there were words
that went deeper than *pain* or *terror*
for the place that woman's eyes can take you
when all you can hear
is the sound the heart makes
with what it knows of itself
and its web of blood.

But right now, the policeman's waiting
for the woman to decide.
That's how he thinks of it; *choice*
or how you can always get what you want
if you want it badly enough.

Everything else he ignores,
like the grip of his own heart's red
persistent warning that he too is fragile.
He thinks he thinks with his brain
as if it were safe up there
in its helmet of bone
away from all that messy business
of his stomach or his lungs.
And when he thinks like that
he loses himself forever.

But perhaps you think I'm being hard on him,
he's only doing his job after all,
only trying to help.
Or perhaps I'm making too much of the heart,
pear-shaped and muscular, a pump really,
when what you want is an explanation or a reason.
But how else can I say it?
Whatever it is you need
is what you must let go of now
to enter your own body
just as you'd enter the room where the woman sat
after it was all over,
hugging her knees to her chest,
holding herself as she'd hold her husband
or their children, *for dear life,*
feeling the arm's limit, bone and muscle,
like the heart's.
Whatever you hear then
crying through your own four rooms,
what you must name for yourself
before you can love anything at all.

LIKE THIS

It's one of those moments we all recognize
sooner or later and always
in the midst of something
so mundane we aren't prepared
to have it open underneath our feet,
become the classic pratfall victims,
Coyote so intent on catching
Roadrunner he doesn't notice
he's walking on air past the edge
of the cliff. Right now we can watch
this man: slim, blond, mid-thirties,
sitting alone at the table, drinking a beer,
reading cookbooks. He's planning a dinner party
– the first one since his separation –
and he wants to use that recipe for
cucumber soup his wife used to make.
It'll be perfect for the meal
he's planned: glazed chicken and rice pilaf.

He can't find it, of course.
It's probably in one of the books she took
or scribbled on a piece of paper, stuck
in the back of a drawer in their old house.

He can also see there's lots of others
worth trying in these books.
He even knows he could call her up
and ask her for the goddamn recipe
if he wanted to.

Which he does.

But won't.

She'd give it to him.
He knows that.
And she wouldn't ask any questions either,
or make any tacky comments.
In fact, she'd probably be really pleased
to think he'd remembered.

And that's just it.
He tries to imagine the conversation, but
the words he'd have to use
and what they might mean
knot in his head
like the fist he feels
in his chest sometimes
when he thinks of her.

When the man hurls his beer bottle
at the kitchen wall,
the explosion of beer and glass
is almost as surprising
as the cry
that splits his throat
at the same time.

We half-expected it, of course,
just as we know that now,
a second later, the wet spot on the wall
begins to look foolish and the puddles
of beer and glass are just another mess
he'll have to clear
before his friends come.

We can see that
even as we understand
how good it felt.

As for the cry
and where it comes from,
we think we recognize that too,
but it won't help. Sooner or later
it'll be our turn. Face up against
the event in our own lives
that can't be expiated
and we'll forget about this man,
this voice we think we hear so
clearly now, saying,
Sorry,
saying, *Look, I've changed.*
Saying, *Isn't that enough?*

Well?

Isn't it?

SPLITTING IT UP

There's only so much anyone can say,
and after that it's almost a relief
to face the quieter expectations
our possessions have of us:
who'll take the wedding lamps, the antique rocker?
The kids' toys, divided in two piles,
one for each household.

In the kitchen, the bottom drawer's stuffed full
of paper bags and bits of tinfoil, waxed paper,
elastic bands. A habit learned from my mother's hands,
smoothing every scrap of a life
where nothing could be wasted.
All forgotten now, like the leftover food
going mouldy in the fridge.
We never could get the hang of it,
children of a richer age, how we hated
our parents' pale obsessions, the weight of things,
their cost, their quality,
their endless, inexplicable uses.

We divide the books and I carry another load
to the porch. Notice how the hinge still sticks
on the front door. I kick it open, awkward thing,
something you could have fixed if you'd wanted to.

It's only now – watching the familiar
duck of your head over a pile of papers,
sorting, choosing – only now I can begin to see
there's only so much anyone can do.
How so much of what we bring to a marriage
has its beginnings far outside our power
to alter or repair, though we bear the burden of it.
Like the hurt we carry away with us,

this furniture we share so scrupulously now,
knowing – though we do not say it –
that it will squat in corners the rest of our lives,
telling its own tales, singing its own histories.

RECLAIMING THE CITY

The sign says, *Windsor, City of Roses,*
but anyone who's lived here knows it's a city of hands
and dark metal, necessary as blood,
or the long lines of cars pumped from its factories
for the arteries of a continent.
A city of days produced on an assembly-line,
the sun an ancient star that doesn't chart things any more,
intruding on the dreams of those who churn with the effort
of learning this tighter chronology.
A city I came to by chance
the way I might meet a man at a party
and talk about anything at all,
never thinking he could change my life forever.
Which is not what I mean to say at all, of course;
a man at a party, putting this stranger in
as a mere figure of comparison
when what I need to say is, *you, you have,*
and what I want from this city now
is a sign, proof that I was a difference.

Tonight, I have dinner with Mark,
still in his apartment by the river.
More than anything, I envy his ease with the place,
love I want to call it, though he doesn't,
shrugging it off with that gesture
I've seen old men use for their wives,
as if what kept them in a marriage all their adult lives
were some paralysis they hadn't found a cure for yet.

He moved here in '67, just before the riots started in Detroit,
his balcony a ringside seat that summer
from which to watch the low hills of smoke
peaked occasionally by sirens or gunfire.
He kept his TV on the railing, tuning in particulars,
the recognizable curve of an arm throwing a bottle,

faces as young as his own, and the others, shielded by rifles
as the army moved in, but he turned the volume off,
he didn't want some newsman to explain things to him,
and now his stories stretch through pauses
more important than the words somehow,
like the fact that he's still sitting here,
taking it all in.

What we study tonight
is how Detroit has rebuilt itself, its skyline
dominated by RenCen, that space-age castle,
a city within a city, where tracks of light are elevators
carrying their passengers high into the night,
though in the older dark below
the planet is reclaiming its own,
block after block, as people move out to the suburbs
the grass moves back, bushes crowd from factories
and trees grow through the rooms of burnt-out houses.
In a few years, Mark says,
RenCen could be stranded in the middle of a forest,
an alien craft, with no-one to remember how it got there,
and tonight even the freighters on the river
move with more than their usual weariness
as if they've known all along
that their cargoes of oil or metal
are the lives of men and women, scrabbled from the earth
one way or another.

In this city where night is always
forcing someone out of bed and into a factory,
dreams come as they will
and if I could travel far enough
I'd find our place on Wyandotte,
just as it was, and you
leaving for work at midnight
while the baby and I curled into sleep,
milky with it, still, in the morning

when you returned, your anger cold as the first light.
All those nights punched in, punched out
to a language I couldn't love you enough to learn.
Any more than you could.
Tuned to your talk of unions and shop-floor politics,
how could you see that I was turning
to another revolution, how our son
tore my days up by their roots
and handed me a life I had to grow to fit
if I wanted to survive.

Statistically, it's common enough. *Marital breakdown*
due to stress. Science leaves us no-one
to blame any more; though in that, how is it different
from politics or religion, our own smaller wisdoms,
whatever brings me back here, hating
what this city made of us and keeps on making
of so many others. *City of Roses,*
though what thrives here is restlessness;
where someone is always working, anything can happen.

And a night like this drives a hard bargain;
it won't let me get away with feeling sorry,
that makeshift emotion I rig up sometimes
to disguise my choices. I'm stuck with what
I can't reclaim: how I loved you
as much as I love my life without you now
or my own body, our marriage in this city
we came to by chance, rooting ourselves
in the child we made, wanting to, not thinking of the future
as he carries us into it.

BLACKFLIES

For Jan Conn

You'd never use that word, of course,
but the one you have is as long as I am
and I can't remember it and anyway
what I really want to tell you is how much
you help me to remember
that language is never neutral.
I like to think it's because
you're both a poet and a scientist,
though all I have to go on, really,
is that peculiar undercurrent
in the rhythm of your speech, a caution
that comes from knowing words and scientific theories
are the tricks we have
for making the world fit
our view of it.

You spend the summer in Guatemala
collecting blackfly larvae and now
you describe your work using the language
of entomology, but they're still
just bugs to me, Jan, the kind that spoil
a weekend at the cottage in early June,
while *vector* and *nematode* place you
in my Grade-13 biology version of a laboratory
where you wear white and dissect things
and this gets all mixed up with
how a friend from Africa told me once
that when she first moved to Ontario it was the bugs
that nearly drove her mad and how surprised I was
because after all she was from *Africa*
where there are snakes that eat people, but
she just laughed and said she didn't
think of it like that.

You don't either.
Onchocerciasis is your word
for river blindness. It makes my skin twitch,
imagining parasites burrowing beneath it,
crawling up my spinal column to my brain
and the backs of my eyes.
A parasite carried by certain blackfly species,
which is the whole point, of course,
though I'm having trouble following you,
want you back in that crisp white lab
with lots of light, but your voice pulls me
out into some river in Guatemala, jungles and heat,
you standing there catching bugs and knowing
It's all useless, you say suddenly.
The government won't give a shit.
It's mainly the Indians who get it, after all.
And now, somewhere beyond you,
people are being shot and in the city
a man works all day for the dollar
that buys some rice or a half-pound of beans
for the children his wife carries
year after year, hoping
that one or two will survive.
It is hard to believe that so small a country
can contain so much horror,
though we never use that word
and *terrorism* is reserved for the bomb
that explodes without warning in a European city.

When you showed me the pictures you'd taken,
I almost laughed. A biologist's view of the place:
closeups of flower-buds and bugs on the undersides of leaves,
a country even smaller than the one my map shows
and more beautiful than it seems it ought to be.
Nothing fits. You spend years finding a cure
for river blindness and in a few quick generations
the parasites will adapt. It's the benefit

of having fewer chromosomes, you've told me,
evolution keeps us all on our toes, a black joke
like the way Chris is always saying
that when we finally kill ourselves off
the insects won't even notice.

For now though, they make me squeamish,
womanish, some might say, a description of my sex
that gets used as a term of derision.
And Jan, don't think this poem is all for you.
It grows out of my own need, this picture
I must invent of you in blue jeans
and a netted hat like the one my aunt wears
when she goes berry-picking.
You in the sweat and heat
moving through the water in that cautious way you have,
keeping your eyes and your hands focused,
your mind on the job.

But even the picture I invent
cannot make you larger,
a stroke as thin as a pencil
or a word against the grey
which I imagine as the colour of that country's sky;
though I know you've told me it is brilliant blue,
in *my* picture, Jan, in *my* picture it's dead
as the eyes of those who follow orders
no matter what they mean, a grey
that drains the colour from the land
until it seems you must raise your hands into fists.

But because this poem is for you, Jan,
that is not what will happen. Instead, I will invent you
bending beneath that sky, into the water
because that is what your job demands,
focusing on what your hand does best
because, like all of us, you must.

WHAT IT COMES TO MEAN

That we take so long to trust
even the most necessary facts,
our lack of power, for one thing,
or the body's patience in teaching us to die.
That we keep on thinking there's a limit
that will make things simple for us,
a once-and-for-all. *I'm done with that,*
my friend says of her divorce, *I've worked it out.*
She believes she can live in the present like that.
We all do.

The summer before Pat died
there was a night at my place
when a bat got in on us. It wouldn't stop
swooping round and round the room.
I had to kill it.
And afterwards, I wanted to stop
every crack in the building, got tape
and a step-ladder, half-crazy, trying to patch out chaos,
Pat on the couch refusing to help,
already knowing that it wouldn't.

I keep looking for a way round this,
an escape, a *worst,*
but even my dreams are houses
only birds find fit to live in,
walls shift and the roof sinks
through dust and wings.

The cries falling back to earth
are thin as the day they bring, another one
that won't protect me any more
from what I don't want to believe:
how every reckoning's a private, ragged thing
that rises, in the seasons of its need,

like Pat's breathing, on her last night,
tearing from the air the only silence
that would fit her, perfect
as her face, which I will never see again.

Sorrow wears itself a hollow,
cleans me out with its crying, a bare voice
like that weather our bones warn us about.
At first I thought it was malevolent,
something that *wouldn't* leave,
but now I know it is no different
from the light that washes in
and brings me my body back, an opening
that finds the people I love, still here,
yawning as they shrug the day on, matter-of-fact
as always, all of us a little puzzled
by our need for each other;

or the way Carolyn takes my hand in the middle of a walk,
laughing, as if it were nothing,
this gentleness we learn
from what we can't heal.

If I had a god,
I'd say we were holy and didn't know it,
but I see only what we make of ourselves on earth,
how long it takes for us to love what we are,
what we offer to each other only in our best moments,
but carelessly, without shyness,
like food grown in plenty,
our mouths blessed with it every day.

MELONS AT THE SPEED OF LIGHT

For Carolyn Smart

"Child," said the lion, "I am telling you your story, not hers. No-one is told any story but their own"
– *C.S. Lewis,* The Horse and His Boy

I keep having this dream
where the women I love swell up like melons, night after night.
It's not surprising, really.
They've reached that age
where a woman must decide once and for all,
and this summer most of them are pregnant.
Already their eyes have changed.
Like those pools you discover once in a while,
so deep with themselves
you can't imagine anything else swimming in them.
The eyes of pregnant women. The women I love
fallen into themselves, somehow, far beyond calling,
as if whatever swims in their bellies
were pulling them deeper and deeper.

I think that women's lives
are like our bodies.
Always at the mercy, you might say.
A woman turns 32 and her body lets her know
it's time to decide.
Or maybe she just loses her job and can't find another,
so she figures she might as well have the babies now as later.
The days become all mouth then
and everything smells of milk.
Her body goes a little vague at the edges
like it felt that time at summer camp
when she was learning how to hang in the water without moving.
"Drown-proofing," they called it.
Said it could hold you up for hours.

These are the days that slow
to the pace of glass,
the world outside a silent, lazy smudge
on the horizon somewhere.
"After my son was born," a friend told me,
"in those first few months, whenever he was asleep,
I'd spend hours putting on makeup,
just so I could touch my own face again,
just so I knew I was there."

In the dreams they are green and determined,
growing larger by the minute, and there's something
I need to warn them about before it's too late,
but they go on ripening without me.
So far, I always find myself awake
before anything else happens,
hands in the dry night, exploring the bed
for a mess of pulp and seeds.
Meanwhile, my son turns ten this summer.
Every morning, he plays baseball in the park next door,
leaving me quiet for coffee and the paper.
But it never works. It's his voice, rising
through the noise of the game, that shapes me still,
the way, years earlier, his turning knotted my belly,
the kick under my ribs, aimed at the heart.
When I take my coffee to the bleachers, he ignores me.
He's the smallest boy on his team, but he's got a good arm.

The coach gives him third base, usually, or shortstop.
Right field is a demotion. I can tell he feels it
by his walk, though his face shows nothing.
It's like the sadness in his wrists when he's up to bat,
knowing he'll manage a good base hit, probably, but never a
  home run.
He's the kind of player every coach needs on the team
and, watching him stretch for a fly ball, I can see
how I'm the one who needs to grow up.

I carried him like the future, unmarked, malleable,
but what I gave birth to isn't like that at all,
isn't a life I can decide for any more.
This is what my son knows already;
he just wants to get on with it.

What I get on with is this dream
where women swell up like melons,
ready to ripen or burst.
I want to believe I am dreaming for my friends,
for all the things I'd tell them if I could.
How they are bound by this birth forever
to the lives of other women, to a love
that roots itself as deeply
as our need for the earth.
I want to tell them this
is an old, old story,
but of course they can't listen.
They are ripening into their own versions of it
as if it had never happened to anyone else before.
These women I love so much.
Their recklessness. Like that fly ball
at the speed of light
stinging into my son's glove.

JEREMY AT TEN

This is the year you will be safest in.
According to statistics, that is,
those talismans I want to trust
like the newborn's caul that midwives saved
against a death by drowning.
This is the year you wear
like an Elven Cloak or Gauntlets of Ogre Power;
this is your Great Tree, your Wind Wailer,
the Bag of Devouring for your travels through the thick,
dangerous forest of my love.

And you are right to think it dangerous.
In our first photograph together,
you're still buried in me,
I am toasting you with a glass of wine,
a riotous madonna, almost as large
as I am in this one
where you hold my knees as I rise
into the sky like a tree,
("like a tree falling," you would tell me
later that year – I was teaching you how to skate
and slipped – "you looked like a tree falling.")
though you can't tell anything from these pictures.
Disguised as mother and son
we could be anybody's,
that's what photographs do,
they deliver us from ourselves
from the darkness their images depend upon.

But there were days when I couldn't stand it.
Your hands on my breasts,
my head filled with nothing
but tears and the smell of urine,
all those days falling in on themselves
one like another, to that afternoon

at the edge of the river, you were throwing stones,
the day I stood behind you thinking
I could push him in and no-one would ever know,
the need flowering as a dream flowers,
filling me with its desire,
a scent I couldn't separate from my own.
How that memory twists my heart,
bloodies my mouth, treacherous
and beautiful as Anat, the goddess
who destroys what she creates,
for this is also how I love you, Jeremy: so much
I could eat you alive.

This is why you must go
now, in the year you will always be
safest in, when the fish spring to your hook
and the earth turns up coins under your feet.
And it will begin in earnest then,
what the midwives mean
with their homely proverb
for every baby a tooth
the first gentle warning
that each birth is also a loss
we never touch the bottom of.

For where else can love be
but in this moment of letting you go, again and again,
the moment when lovers turn from each other at last
or the child turns to begin its journey into light,
the moment when we know ourselves to be unique,
mortal, separate, like everybody else,
the tips of our tongues, Jeremy,
each strand of hair,
our cells as constant as the stars
burning with their necessary song.

LEARNING FROM THE HANDS

They say it's in the opposition of the thumbs.
For all we know, whales sing in five-act plays,
but they can't write them down.
In a few million years – our wings slimming into arms
or paws flexing to fingers – we've made great strides
in the animal kingdom, most of it on our hands.

Some hands can see.
Those of the blind, of course, the delicate whorls
of their fingertips shining like eyes,
and maybe those of certain healers,
though perhaps it's more like sonar guides them
to the cells' cry for help; the hands of potters, definitely,
and wood-carvers, old men who can free
fantastic animals from glum wood;
but mostly hands, being hands, insist
that touch is the first mystery, wiser than sight.
Everywhere pregnant women place a hand to the belly,
listening for the first flutter-kick, the child inside
rocked by the warm walls of its mother's body,
stronger, even, than the sound of her heart.

All our lives, the hands of strangers feed us
and closest to our skin we wear
whatever their hands have learned, the small humiliations
they carry in to work with them each day.
We deliver ourselves to the hands of doctors
and carpenters, engineers, pilots, dentists, cab-drivers,
some guy tightening bolts on an assembly-line somewhere
stoned or hungover, angry at his foreman,
in love with the new girl in payroll
or just plain bored, we trust him
with our lives every time we start the car.
No wonder jugglers and magicians say
that magic is in the hands,

which are never really quicker than the eye,
only more sure of themselves.

This is how we live,
in a world run by thugs
who think a hand is just a weapon,
like the body, a machine for following orders,
filling the fields and oceans of the earth
with the ones that have refused.
This is what hands have become
after so many centuries, having to learn
how much they can endure
before the nerve-ends underneath the fingernails
stop screaming at the brain.
And something else the hands know
only too well: how often they must measure
the little they can do
against how long it takes.
We each carry our life in our hands –
the palm's cartography unfolded
for the fortune-teller, as if the future mattered –
our deaths, which belong to us from the beginning,
visible, necessary as the past
which nothing can take from us, ever.

There are nineteen small bones in the hand
and nineteen small muscles. *Eight muscles*
are inserted into the bones of the thumb.
All are used in combination
and all movements of the thumb are complex.
They can gouge a mountain,
put an eye back in its socket;
they are the needles thought needs to piece
the world together, the brain's light
threaded through the thumb;
or the heart's – hands are the only arrows
of desire that can reach what they want,

they mean what they can do
and no more, taking so many million years
to bring us here, our hands
what we have instead of wings,
the closest we can come to flight.

The Stubborn Particulars of Grace

Possibility and limitation mean about the same thing.
– *Flannery O'Connor*

APPEAL

That family joke every Sunday,
all of us for dinner at Grandma's
and my dad asked to give thanks
always mumbling into his plate
and my grandmother always looking up
to say "I didn't hear half of that,"
and my dad always replying "Well, Mother,
I wasn't just talking to you."
The laugh that followed
so predictable, so necessary
that the whole thing sang in my mind,
joined the steaming bowls and platters
moving hand to hand above my head
with the slow, clean words
my aunts and uncles used
to make an anecdote or a bit of gossip
into the story of their lives, that world
I found mysterious as their names became
when I looked at their faces or their arms.

When I look at my mother
on a night in 1953, or maybe '55,
sitting on the lawn at the cottage
with my dad and Frank and Helen, the Americans
from across the lake, who've come over
with a bottle of gin and some Marlboros,
which my father is enjoying, though my mother,
her posture what Protestantism becomes
when the protest's gone, sits prim and uncomfortable.
I'm inside, trying to sleep,
but you can tell it's too hot by how the sheet's
already clinging to my legs, itching
like the bites on my arms, the whine
of another mosquito in here somewhere,
the air so close my mother's voice

comes right in – "OK, Frank, give me
one of those things; maybe the smoke'll
keep these bugs away!" – bringing my head
up to the window-sill, to her face
laughing in the match flare, tip
of the cigarette that lights my father's
face and Frank's and Helen's too
glints off glass and the metal
rim of lawn chairs. Even the lake
stops nudging the dock for a minute,
lets the night come in, as it can
maybe once, twice, in the whole summer,
when the dark fills up that hot, still air
with something close to clarity.

But what can I call that glimpse
I had then? Or explain why it shines
from my mother still, sets off
what I love in her? How the look
on my father's face (that look,
I see now, that happens when those we love
reveal, as they did the first time,
something we thought we'd lost
to the work of simply getting by)
burns through my memory, lights up
whatever I know of their marriage, of the weariness
and caring and surprise that brought me here
and from which I watch my own kid
take his bearings from some act of mine,
caught briefly, at a distance
further than that night seems now.

A night I offer you, those faces
cupped by darkness, lake and shoreline
as a hand cups a match for the moment
it is needed, even in a light wind,
unable to tell you more or why.

Caught, as I used to be,
by that trick an aunt or uncle'd use
of always stopping right at the best part
to take a bite of pie, a sip of tea,
their way of leaning back to look
around the table, let the story sink right in.
As if they hoped to find
that opening in each of us
from which, long after we'd been told
what happened next, they could begin
their slower, more miraculous
returns.

Joseph MacLeod Daffodils

HOUSES

For Jim Rhodes

A woman looks up from her after-dinner coffee
to the garden where her husband leans
checking his broccoli, the curve of his bum
something she's still in love with
after all these years. Scarlet runner beans
climb the bamboo trellises he's built for them,
crazy trees, like the ones that rose
from his discovery that melons could grow
upright, each fruit supported by a muslin sling,
brassieres the neighbours called them,
but it worked, and the woman sees all this
(sees yellow marigold among the purple
stems of beet leaves, red nasturtiums
curling through the lettuce patch)
framed by a kind of generosity
she thought only painters had,
while a block away, in the upper half
of a stucco duplex, a young graduate student
has just met her new roommate's boyfriend,
a market analyst from Ottawa, whose sister,
it turns out, is married to a doctor, Peter
Mathewson, the same Peter Mathewson
the graduate student went to kindergarten with
in Thunder Bay, twenty years ago. "I can't
believe it," she keeps saying, as she pours
more wine, "I really can't believe it,"
though what choice does she have?
It's a small world and, besides, it's
the only life she'll get, a fact
that her neighbour, three doors up,
is also coming to, and hating
as he hates how his wife has to help him
out of the car and up the stairs, into bed.

"A minor operation," the doctor told him,
but that's not what the man feels now
as he curls around this new pain, this absence
of some part of himself he'd never even
thought about, ignorant as most of us are
of what really goes on in there.

Or maybe that's not it
at all. Maybe the woman glares
over her cup, hating the old fool, fussing
and fussing with his goddamn plants, the dead
white strip of skin between his shirt and
his trousers as he bends reminding her
of everything she can't love anymore
and he can't change, like the ache
she feels in her joints these nights
when the rain gets in and brags of its power there;
maybe Peter Mathewson married a stewardess, won
a lottery, moved to Monaco, maybe the boyfriend's
a sexist jerk who farts at the table.
The graduate student looks at her roommate
again. The couple up the street come home
with their new twins, his parents meet them
at the door with armloads of yellow roses,
the exact same yellow as the babies' blankets,
the lawn chairs in the yard next door, the shorts
on the young girl watching from across the street;
"I don't believe it," someone murmurs, as the door
swings shut, leaving the words alone, outside
the houses in which lights are turned on, drinks
spilled, letters started, baths run, where a man
calls out over the rush of water or his own thoughts
to whatever he thinks his wife just asked him
from the next room. "Of course," he hollers,
"of course I do!"

FAST CARS

For John & Lindy Stevenson

I liked how you arrived
for dinner last night, your arms
full of roots and cuttings for my garden,
how the music I was playing brought out
some crazy incident from your high-school days
so that soon we were all telling: first, those parts
we think we're old enough to laugh at now
and later, all that other stuff,
what Flannery O'Connor was getting at
when she said that "anybody who has survived his childhood
has enough information about life
to last him the rest of his days."
(How she should know,
her own life narrowed
to the distance she could cover
on crutches, on the farm
where her mother cared for her
and her stories grew, grace
like the brilliant turquoise of her peacocks,
widening before our eyes.)

I don't know how long
we sat that night. On the back porch
the plants leaned out through the dark
to the next day, the earth I'd turned
ready for them. But I know it was late
when we reached our own children,
all of them eager
to head off into whatever we fear
will take them furthest from us.
Booze or secrets. Sex. Fast cars.
How these things worry us, even as we know
that theirs may be the last generation

of kids on earth, our hearts contracting,
as they must, to what they think
they can comprehend.

After you'd left, I thought of a story
I hadn't told and how it fit with one I had:
when I was twelve, my best friend's brother Roger,
sixteen and drunk, went through the windshield
of his friend's Volkswagen two days before Christmas.
Six months later, the presents were still there,
unopened, on their hall shelf, and for years
my dad went on and on about German cars,
how dangerous they were,
another rant I had to tune out
with the rest of his war stories.
But if Freud's right about anything,
then it wasn't an accident
my first boyfriend drove one. Yellow.
That was the boy I told you about.
Doug, of the green eyes, who took me to a beach
that smelled of lemons for no reason at all,
the boy who taught me to drive the twisty road
to the highway, both of us pissed to the gills
all that summer when I got neither killed
nor pregnant and my father didn't know.
Didn't know as he glared from the doorway
every evening when Doug picked me up
and we drove off laughing.

And that's where we left him last night.

It's only remembering that other car, that
other child, that I can turn to find my father
smaller now, his thin shoulders rounded
as if to protect his chest and the knowledge

he has to keep there, as we all do,
for himself. Me, just driving into it then.
And him, just letting me go.

No. I should have said
having to.

THE WATERMELON INCIDENT

It was during this same summer,
in the back seat of another
speeding car, that I nearly
cut my finger off, slicing watermelon
with a jack-knife. We were all laughing
when the knife went in
to the bone, when it sucked out
one of those silences through which
blood spurted over my hand and onto the
watermelon, onto my other hand, my
knees, staining my new black and white
checked pedal-pushers which my mother said
were too tight anyway, made me look
cheap, like the peroxide streaks
Lorraine and I put in our hair when she
was babysitting at the Neilsons', onto
the grey plush seat and down to my
ankle socks, to my white sandals, onto
the floor, until Lorraine said "Jesus
H. Christ," and the car pulled over
rolled to a stop where we all got out
and stared. Two miles away,
the city bristled with hospitals,
antiseptic, doctors, cat-gut,
parents and tetanus shots, but we
were Beyond All That. Immortal.
And it's because I mean this
literally
that the bleeding stopped
that the end of my finger hung,
by a strand, from the rest of it
that Lorraine found some bandaids
she'd stuffed in her purse in case
her new shoes gave her blisters
that they held

that my mother was cooking dinner
when I got home
that my brother poked me in the ribs
and chewed with his mouth full
that nobody asked
that it was after the sun went down
(and in that sudden way a sunburn
will) that the pain surfaced.

Through my sleep, my hand
the size of a boxing glove
as if all the blood still in my body
pushed to that spot
where the bandaids held me together
and on whatever cool square
of sheet or pillow
I could find for it
kept it up: *pound-pound, pound-pound*
pound-pound, pound-pound,
until I knew for sure
it'd wake my parents
sleeping in the next room.

I'm one of those people
who believe that we remember
everything, though we may not know it.
Just the other day, in fact, I read
that even though we forget what we learn
when we're drunk, it'll all come back
sometime, when we're drunk again.
And that made me think
of the guy who lived in the apartment next
to the place I had before my son was born,
one of those buildings where so much
has passed from one room to another
that the walls thin out,
like those spots in an old shirt

where grease or sweat's been scrubbed at
so that the skin shines through,
so that every Friday night, when this guy
got drunk, I could hear the bottles
dropping, empty, to the table top
and by the tenth, maybe, the twelfth,
he'd be on to his mother, how he'd
disappointed her, he'd start wailing
and pounding the walls. Most of the time
I hated him, this old fart, sobbing
in his beer for Mama. I'd turn
the TV up or go for a walk,
but other nights, I guess, he must have
got in with my own sounds, somehow,
like those bits of dreams you never
quite let go, until this thing
I read on drunkenness and memory
opens the door for him and he sings there,
fiercely, in the midst of all the other stuff
about the watermelon and the knife
missing it, the blood and Lorraine's face,
the pain pounding out from my finger
to my wrist to my chest to my throat, my teeth
clenched over it, my parents
sleeping, soundly, on.

ONE OF THE THINGS I DID BACK THEN

Funny what returns and how you can't predict
what you'll use it for,
how the smell that means summer to me
isn't roses or freshly mown grass
but that hot-baked dusty steam
that rises from the pavement
just after the street cleaner's gone, gritty
and warm as any memory worth the work:
so a little girl stands
at the curb's edge in her bathing suit
catching the fine spray, the wave
from the driver.

How that memory leads me
to another. It's 1968 and I am standing
in the sweaty basement of the library, smelling
the must and mildew of old newspapers, the dust
coating my fingertips as I search
the birth announcements for 1948, '49,
checking them off against the deaths
and when I find one (*someone,* who died
in infancy) I write his name, the dates
on a card, and go on
to the next stack of papers.

Somewhere, someone else
who is 19 or 20
waits for this information.
Perhaps he is at my apartment sleeping
or drinking beer in my kitchen. Perhaps
he is walking nervously in the park or
riding a bus into town. Perhaps
he is still in the jungle, half a world
away, in Vietnam, trying to figure out
how to get here, though he doesn't know

where "here" is yet. No matter.
When he deserts,
his real name becomes a skin
he has to shuck, so he can wear
the one I'll give him, a dead child's,
that allows him a birth certificate,
a social insurance number, a chance.

The rest comes in pieces.
All that stuff I saw later,
changed into movies – the young men
pushed from helicopters, the children
bursting into flames – I met then
for the first time, a war
coming at me, not from the TV
but through my own front door, born from hands
that dried dishes or made soup, carried
my groceries in from the car, from faces
belonging to guys who'd refused their deaths
as they'd tried to refuse the lives
they'd been doled out, always hoping
something better would turn up.

Mostly I see what I did back then
as a way I had to help them,
but sometimes I think about the parents
of the babies whose names I stole, how they'd feel
if they knew and whether it was a kind of violation.
I remember the excitement
of finding each one, like winning a lottery,
and how the names, the two dates
made the cards I used
look a little like tombstones,
those "letters of recommendation
to the dead," Berger has called them,
"… written in the hope that they,
who have left, will not need to be renamed."

Here, we know only too well
the chances a name offers
or denies. The difference it can make,
like the bit of luck or the casual decisions
that add up to a lifetime.

Here, I know, too, that the war
I thought I had a tiny part in stopping
merely shifted location and goes on
as planned.

And once, I remember,
I went back to June 2, 1945,
found my own birth,
announced with everything else,
proof of my own passing
into history, the future, my place
in the world and what
I would make of it.

GIFTS

Right now, my son is crying
because the T-shirt he bought me for my birthday
is a bit too small.
He has flung himself on his bed
and his sobs carry him out
and further away from me,
the sound of them sinking
into the noise of the party downstairs
like the stubborn intervals
that try to force a song apart.

As for the shirt, it's not that small
and I'd wear it anyway,
because of the Mickey Mouse decal
he's had put on and my name, too,
because he saved up for it
because I'm his mother
and he's my child, all that corny truth
that would have been enough
even a year ago
and isn't now.
He can see for himself how it wrinkles
under the armpits and clings
to my shoulder-blades.
He can see it's not my style,
just as he knows he can't exchange it.
Can't take it back   can't take it back;
it's the chill of that,
laying its damp yellow touch
on the fine brown arm of his love
for years to come,
like the words we let fly
in the midst of an argument,
how they natter, dry birds,
in some empty room of the brain.

It seems all summer I have watched
this growing in him, seen it rise,
unbidden as that gesture he has for impatience,
my own, made with his father's hands.
Seen it glistening like oil on his skin
as he measures himself for the world,
studying how the older boys
dive from the raft at the cottage
and then, alone, practising all morning
just as his dad might concentrate
on the tongue and groove of a shelf, the slide
of a desk drawer, a perfect fit.
But when the big boys
rocked the raft until it flipped,
a huge thing, coming down
in a crash of water, shouts
from the beach, I saw him
in the shallows with the younger kids,
small against that spinning instant
when you'd have to jump free
or get your head bashed in
(how you'd have to be sure
you could, sure
as you could be)
saw the grey pinch of his cheeks
as he entered this knowledge
the way he'd enter
any other element, that first breath
that took him from me
stinging his lungs,

or when, as now
he returns for a while
from wherever his crying took him,
grinning up at me in this crazy shirt,
the cost of it already pinned to his chest
an old badge, so that soon

we will return together to the party
which is for my birthday, the day
when we begin to learn all this,
taking a lifetime just to recognize ourselves
and one day
from that whole terrible journey
to celebrate it.

JOSEPH MACLEOD DAFFODILS

for Isabel Huggan

"I'm planting perennials this year," you tell me,
"because I'm scared and it's the only way I know
to tell myself I'm going to be here,
years from now, watching them come up."
Maybe it's a phase we're going through,
since I'm at it too; lily of the valley,
under the back hedge, thinking *when Jeremy*
is old enough to drive, I'll have to divide these,
put some under the cedars there; by the time
he leaves home, they'll be thick as grass,
and at the same time saying
"God, we're parodies of ourselves,
sixties children, still counting on flowers,
for chrissake, to get us through."
Knowing you'll see it that way too,
your snort of laughter
the index of my love and the wisdom
of George Eliot's observation that
"a difference of taste in jokes
is a great strain on the affections."
(Another thing we share, our delight
in quotations like that, exactly what you'd expect
from girls who grew up wearing glasses
into women who read everything;
your bathroom so much like mine,
a huge bin of books by the toilet
and on the shelves, all the bottles
turned label side out.
"The contents of somebody's bathroom,"
Diane Arbus said, "is like reading their biography.")

This doesn't help much, does it?
You're laughing, but your hands stay

clenched in your lap, still forcing
the tight, dumb bulbs into the ground
as if you could force your life
to a pattern as serene as theirs,
a calm that flourishes in darkness
to the pull of the sun.
Still, I keep on talking.
It's the only wisdom that I've got.
How about this one: you know those
big, yellow daffodils – they're called
Joseph MacLeods – well, the way they got their name
was that the man who developed them
always kept a radio on in the greenhouse
and the day the first one bloomed, in 1942,
was the day he got the news
of the Allied victory, against Rommel,
at El Alamein, and the announcer who read the news
was Joseph MacLeod. Which shows a sense of history
I can appreciate; no *El Alamein Glorias* or
Allied Victory Blooms for this guy, you can be sure.
It's like the story my mother always tells
about joining the crowds on V-E day, swollen with me,
but dancing all night, thinking *now*
she can be born any time.

What I love
is how these stories try to explain
the fit of things, though I can see
your mood's for something more sinister.
Like the reason Diane Arbus gave
for photographing freaks, maybe?
"Aristocrats," she called them,
"they've already passed their test in life."
Being born with their trauma, that is,
while the rest of us must sit around, dreading it.
Meaning you and me. *Normal.* Look at us,
practically wizened with worry, hunched

over coffee cups, whispering of cancer and divorce,
something happening to one of the kids, our lives
spread between us like those articles you read
about Mid-Life Crisis or Identity Anxiety,
Conflict of Role Expectations in Modern Marriages,
the kind that tell you you can fix all that
with less red meat and more exercise,
the ones that talk as if the future's
something you decide about,
though what it all comes down to, every time,
is making do. You can call it a choice
if you want, but that doesn't change
what we learn to rely on,
the smaller stratagems. Whatever works.
The socks in their neat balls, tucked on the right
side of the drawer, the iris coming up each summer
in the south bed. "Be sincere and don't fuss."
"Noble deeds and hot baths
are the best cures for depression."

It's what I love in you, Isabel.
How you can stand here saying
"Brave and kind. I want to get through this
being brave and kind," squaring your shoulders
like a heroine in those movies our mothers watched
where people knew their problems
didn't amount to a hill of beans
in this crazy world and let it go at that,
fitting themselves to the shape
a life makes for itself without meaning to.
I love your grin from the end of my sidewalk
as you head for home, posed like a photograph.
"Perfectly Ordinary Woman on Suburban Street."
"A secret about a secret," Arbus called this kind,
"the more it tells you,
the less you know."

Testimonies

THE MAN WITH THE SINGLE MIRACLE

Here is a man whose life surrounds him
like a house outgrowing its owner.
Surrounds, but doesn't protect. This isn't
safety I'm describing, here
where the morning light gets in
on the sly, prowls around the edges,
sniffing out the dust
before it gathers enough of itself
to pounce. He never gets used to it.
There's always that moment when he can't remember,
when he imagines he's been brought here
drugged, at night, by strangers,
even his hands grown part of some mechanized nightmare,
tools he only operates, but doesn't understand
as they reach for his clothes, the smell and texture
what his body takes for reassurance.

Of course you know the sort of guy I mean,
with a job he likes enough to keep,
a wife he thinks of as his best friend
and kids who seem to be having
the sort of lives he'd hoped they would.
Like all of us, right, this man
whose jaw tightens in the sad part of a movie
though he knows it's really schmaltzy,
who believes they'll find a cure for cancer
before he gets it and assumes that his friends
are much like himself, wary of the way the days grow up
hodgepodge, like those places you find on the backroads
where no one bothers to plan anything.

This is why he is glad when they get together,
drinks and cigarettes, the stories they tell, he loves it
when someone just starts off slowly,
their voice as tentative as a kid's fingers

tracing line and squiggle on a page
till DOG or CAT leaps from the paper
in a sudden widening of the eyes.
He loves how his friends build their lives
into stories like that; even he has one
he tries to tell, though it never comes out right.
It's about the witch
who lived at the corner of his street
when he was eight and he always begins with her house
which you couldn't see for all the shrubs and trees
so he tries to explain how it felt, how the air thickened
and the sidewalks narrowed to a breath
you had to squeeze through on your way to the corner store.
At least he wants to make it that slow and heavy,
but his voice always sticks to his heart somehow
and the next thing he knows it's raced right on
to the part where he finds himself
in her kitchen, just staring at her
sitting there in her rocking chair
and how the thing he notices first
is that she is drinking milk
straight from the carton,
sort of pouring it down her throat
the way he does when his mother isn't around,
and he doesn't even know why this is so important,
but it is, so he tries to show them
how it goes with the smell of oilcloth and
onions – that was it – and how that smell fitted
the worn patch of linoleum under her chair,
a patch that warmed to the round, stinging
bite his dime made in his clenched fist.
Except that none of this comes out right
because before he's even finished
his friends start trying to figure out
how he got into the house in the first place;
but once they get going on dreams

or astral projection or some crazy theory
he never has a chance
to tell about being back on the street again
in front of the store, his ice cream
already oozing over his fingers;
or how just as he plunges into it, he raises his eyes
to where the road up ahead ripples and shines,
the whole city gone liquid, rushing
to the tip of his tongue.

You can see his problem, can't you?
And you can see how hard it would be,
getting together with his friends
on Saturdays for drinks and a couple of laughs.
Even the words he'd need, for one thing, belong
in the faces of those creatures
every city tolerates, their ramblings,
if they ever get you to listen,
nearer to prayers than anything else.
Besides, he loves his friends. Even this need
for explanations is something he feels tender about;
how can he help letting them rummage through his story,
the new owners of a place he can't keep up anymore.

This man I'm telling you about
lives in a city near a lake and by January
the harbour's usually frozen over
so that the people who live on the island, two miles out,
start driving to work instead of lining up for the ferry.
Pretty soon there's a good-sized road packed down
where someone in a truck has marked the treacherous spots
with oil drums or old Christmas trees,
though there's hardly a year goes by
that a car doesn't go through.
The city council tries to pass by-laws
forbidding cars on the lake, but by then

everyone's out there, so what can you do.
His kids love it, and every Sunday
they beg to go walking to the island.

Once in a while, he can feel the ice shift under him, more
like sound than motion, how it heaves up
from his feet to his throat, and though he knows
there's no real danger, what he trusts most is
that everyone else is out there too.

Only sometimes, this gets all mixed up, crazy,
like at a party when he'll feel that same
rise and swell pressing into his lungs,
when he looks over at his wife,
laughing in the corner there
or at someone else starting,
a little unsteadily,
towards the kitchen,
and he wants to call to them,
but he can't, any more than he can believe
what he sees; how their deaths
quicken the air around them, stipple their bodies
with a light like the green signals
trees send out before their leaves appear.
All right, he *won't* believe it then,
but doesn't it come to the same thing
for all of us? So frail, how could we bear
this much grace, when it glances
off the odds and ends we've no idea
what to do with, the jumble we just can't
throw out, stuffed into rooms
full of corners, old women
with cartons of milk at their lips
rocking back and forth.

FAMILIARS

That they should come back now,
to this part of my life
and not just through dreams either,
but sidling into daythoughts
with the same unerring timing that they mastered
was it fifteen, no, twenty years ago.
Those two. Zed and Zelda
I called them. For a joke,
though they came to fit their names
or maybe their names, like anyone else's,
came to mean what they were, how
can you tell?
Zed was just that – lean and abrupt,
determined too; I used to imagine her
chain-smoking and giving orders, like Joan Crawford
in *Mildred Pierce.* If there was anything wrong
with the food, Zed let me know, for both of them,
while Zelda sat around grooming herself
all day, always pretty and fluffy, outside
and in, a real airhead; she could have starred
in every beach party movie ever made.
I called her Zelda because I couldn't imagine her
without Zed there, and everyone thought
it was so cute, how she snuggled up to Zed
at night and licked her ears, while Zed kept
one paw around her shoulders, always.
Cute, we all said, how they loved each other
like the kittens on a calendar,
like those cartoon shows
where cats and mice and rabbits
are really humans in disguise
as if the thought of their being anything else
were far too lonely for us to bear.

When Zelda died, Zed found the body.
And after that, she sat in their box
with her face to the wall, howling;
I want to say crying, but that's
wrong too, just as my trying to tell you
how she went skittish and grey, crazy-eyed
like someone on speed, won't explain it either
and anyway, she left about then
so that I only saw her in the alleys
or around the garbage by the pizza place,
though once, a year later, she came back
limping and, well, hardened somehow.
to sit in her old spot for a while
looking out this time, at me
from a distance wider than any
a common language could have filled.

And she's back again. I can feel it,
just as I think I see some of her look
in the one I'm getting
from my own son these days, the one
he brings out during the argument
we're always having, the argument
neither of us can ever win
(and which winning wouldn't matter anyway)
the one that began with his first word
and slowly clarifies itself, like a photograph
in a developing tray, what my son holds up
as evidence: the life he sees
out there, away, in the future.
At 13, he carries
the little I've had time to give him
easily, just as I hope he'll lose,
someday, the weight of my failings
which are heavy now, like the scorn
he bears me. *I love you* I say to him
I love you, almost afraid,

like when I was a kid and believed
you could only use a word so many times
before it flickered out, a flashlight
with a dead battery.

So, lots of times I talk to him
inside my head, though I don't like to.
It's too much like the conversations
I catch myself having
with a friend who's died, when I want to say
you and mean it, unable to believe
I can't anymore, just as I can't imagine
her body, sunk through death
until the earth's become the only air
it rakes in and releases, more slowly,
more surely, year after year.
This is the power she'll have for me
always. As my son will.
It's why the cats are back. Those two,
Zed and Zelda, and then just Zed,
that crazy grey cat out there, past
the reach of our comfort, our human
laughter, that other animal
come back, in broad day, to sit
in this room with me and stare
from across it all.

BENEDICTION

for Peter D.

The unexpected rituals that grow
out of an ordinary life, like those acts
which by their constant repetition
fix themselves in the cells, the muscles
folding more than we remember
into their layers of tension and release,
just as the objects we possess
may tell the stories of our lives
more accurately than we ourselves could.

A wedding ring and the art
of making pastry are all I have
from our marriage, Peter.
The one's almost too small for my finger now,
but the other's a rite by which I am returned
each time I perform it
to that first, crazy summer,
all the wasted flour and tears
cursing cookbooks and rolling pins
until (like making bread, like
riding a bicycle) it arrived
to live in my fingertips, my brain,
so that each pie I make
recalls that first perfect one
set down before you, recalls
the young bride and the year
that cut so deeply into my life
it found its way to my palmline, the mark
each fortune teller notices, right off,
before everything else,
that means I can't explain you
easily, the way I want to, with
some dumb cliché about children
playing house.

And that makes this news of your death
come too hard, damn it.
A voice I don't know on the telephone
says *cancer* says *peacefully*
and you're gone. Like that.
As if they'd taken my favourite photograph
– the one in the churchyard after the wedding
where I'm leaning against you, laughing –
and pulled you out of it,
so that I pitch backwards
wildly, my face convulsed
like a fool's or a drunkard's.

To imagine how I came
to this. My name on a list
you've made, probably, its writing
a time-travel as you moved through it
into that wider space
the dying need for their work.

I say "the dying" and mean you,
Peter. Each death specific
as the terms that bind me to it,
so that yours, which looses
the cells of your body, scatters
the details of our marriage too, the bits
that matter to no one else
I'd meant to gather in some day,
the address of our place on King Street,
and that couple downstairs
– the people we went to Mexico with –
her name was Helen, what was his?
                                        I miss you
more now. So young then, I thought forever
came with words, the hateful things
we never took back, not knowing
some people could and go on somehow

as if nothing had happened. How I said
I never wanted to see you again
and believed it, the way I believed
in childhood as a simple time
I'd passed through, dreaming,
into what I imagined
was a life of my own.

So I keep coming back to that list,
how my name must have brought you
into our life again, unseen,
already a ghost. Though who knows
how we reach each other, what ceremonies
will appease, when something so commonplace
as easy as pie will have to do for us. Will serve
as the touch to the tightened muscle
that loosens anger or grief, my voice
sent out to you at last
with its small song of forgiveness.

And how that too will be returned,
always, now, to me
who can still use it.

TESTIMONIES

for Julie Cruikshank

As the cadence in an old woman's voice
becomes the line that will lead others
into the territory her people saw,
you make me see
the importance of your work, the long hours
taping these languages which only a few
of the elders speak now. "My stories are my wealth,"
one woman tells you, "all I have to give
my children," and you help create the alphabet
that takes them there. Linguistic anthropology,
the science of making language
into maps. The crazy detours
it can take you on, that story
of the parrot up in Carcross, N.W.T.,
a bird someone brought over the pass
during the gold-rush and left at the Caribou Hotel
where it lived for another sixty years
entertaining customers by singing
nineteenth-century bar-room ballads
in a cockney accent. The voice of a dead miner
kept on in a brain the size of an acorn,
all the countries of his lifetime, contracted
to its bright, improbable presence
amid men who figure they've seen
just about everything now,
so that their sitting there, listening like that
becomes part of the story too,
just as I am added when I tell it,
as anyone will be, each version
a journey that carries us all along,
as the shards of pottery, carefully labelled
and carried up through layered villages
flesh out more hands
than the two that made them.

How can any of us know
what will speak for us or who
will be heard? We who are never
satisfied, eager for the evidence
no matter how it comes, slowing the car down
as we pass the accident, to see
what's pulled from the wreckage, crowding
the ones who were at the scene, the cop
or the ambulance driver, the survivors
stepping forward for their moment, blessed
by our terrible need to know everything.
Even those women we dread
sitting next to on buses or trains,
their bodies swelling with messy secrets,
the odour of complaint on their breath,
may be prophets. Whether we listen or not
won't stop them from telling
our story in their own.

Not far from where I live, a man ploughs
someone's skull up in his cornfield
and the next spring, four more, a family maybe
though no one knows even that,
their being there at all,
and longer, the only claim that's offered.
Like the farms themselves, their few rich fields
the chance deposits of a glacier.
Even the ones that I keep looking for,
wading through goldenrod to a house
where just inside the door, the trunk of old clothes
or the chair that didn't make it
to the load on back of the truck
bears witness to those smaller choices
we all have to make
about the future
and what can be wisely carried into it.

What your work brings you to, I see now,
not the past. Each site, a threshold
into this slow discovery,
the random testimony gathered
as best we can, each of us down
to essentials, as the failed are
and the dead, who bear us forward
in their fine, accurate arms.

FOOD

for Marty, and in memory of Jessie Glaberman

Begin where we all do
with milk. How I still like mine
straight from the cow, driving out
to a farm each week, through fields
dotted with Holsteins, the only landscape
I can understand. My dad says the stuff
that's really worth drinking's
squirted warm and straight from the teat
and I believe him, just as I know
his city life's the instrument
that pries that memory loose
from the history he hated, the narrow
caked path from pasture to barn
and the blistered sun at his neck
day after day. Just as I know
for me, too, it's more nostalgia
in the glass, as even the smallest farms
become factories, the cows hooked up
from udder to tank to truck
to pasteurization plant
and on (in just a few years, probably)
to what's become of beef or chicken, things
kept in buildings never opened to the sun.

Food. Or the politics of food. You see
I did learn what you tried to teach me, you two:
your house on Bewick Avenue, your table
where a union man from Bologna might meet up
with a woman from a feminist commune
in New Mexico or a kid from Oregon, on the road
for the summer, who'd heard about your place,
everybody hashing out their differences
over meals that went on for as long

as our appetites lasted and the wine held,
Jessie at her end, pushing her glasses up
with one hand, passing food with the other,
Marty at his, finger out, making some
theoretical point someone else had overlooked,
living up to the joke we made of his habit,
as soon as he'd open his mouth, we'd laugh
and call out, "and then Lenin said ..."
loving him for it.

Just as I love you, Marty,
for that whole hot summer
when you taught me to read *Capital*
of all things, as I thought no book
could be read, cold theory warmed
by those hands of yours, the lines
that oil and grit had eaten there
part of what you were saying, just as the smell
that clings to hair and clothes gives off
the heat of a factory, the noise,
fights with foremen, meetings, wildcats,
always at it, "The working class
is revolutionary or it is nothing" – Karl Marx.
"But not a slogan," I can hear you saying,
"a statement of fact; either we'll manage
to change things or we'll disappear,"
your finger out as you say this, the other hand
reaching for chicken or coffee, refusing
to separate food from what it costs.

Jessie, in the only snapshot I have
your mouth's open, of course, your face
blurred by what you were saying at the moment,
words freed as carelessly as the smoke
from your cigarettes, filling the air
and disappearing. At your end of the table
everything was always up for grabs;

"Spit it out," you'd cry, when we fumbled
for a straighter phrase, "don't be afraid
to say what isn't finished, what seems
crazy. Just say what you can;
we'll look at it together."
And we would. All of us,
peering into those dimmer, tangled
regions theory doesn't open on
and though I bet we'd argue still
about what got said those nights,
we'd all be hearing your voice
angry, laughing, leading us into them.
Oh, Jessie, it drives me crazy
knowing you died alone,
how you must have hated, struggled
and in another movement,
taken it, knowing we are always
alone in this, your shrug
– I can see it still – what I have
of you, your work
that widening of the wild zone
between the power to fight what happens to us
and the power to accept what is.

It's late afternoon in the old house on Bewick.
In the kitchen, someone's poking around
trying to decide what to have for dinner,
while in his new apartment
Marty follows an argument about Poland
from the stove, where he's making
his famous stir-fry, a recipe
I'll use myself tonight, with tomatoes
and zucchini from my garden, snow peas
from the guy in the third stall, second row
at the market, soy and ginger, Basmati rice
from I don't know where, and while we eat
I'll tell my family how I heard

on the radio today the future's
in kiwi fruit, a new type, hairless
and the size of grapefruit, more vitamin C
than a dozen oranges and easier to ship.
I'll tell them how scientists
have developed an apple tree
shaped like a telephone pole, no branches,
fruit straight from the stem, for easier
picking and bigger profits and while we
take this in, women I've eaten with
are adding sour cream and red wine
to their pot roasts, as Jessie
taught them to. For all I know,
they're quoting Lenin and Marx,
maybe the FBI is right, subversion
is everywhere.
Oh, I know, I know, it's late
in the century, the revolution hasn't come,
the hungry go on, food costs the earth,
the work of getting enough
breaks us all, I know, I know,
but even so, the tomatoes
are red, ready to sting
my tongue, the smell of their vines
clings to my arms, Marty talks
with his mouth full, his finger
urgent as always, a woman throws
a handful of parsley in the pot, a taste
brings me up to her, and it's that
I'm telling for the moment, just
for now.

ANNIVERSARY

in memoriam, Pat Logan

The road turns off
just where it always does and rising
comes out to the second corner
where the graveyard is.
Your grave. You. Behind us,
in one of those reforestation stands
the government plants, the pines
grow taller in their narrow columns
as if to show me how there can be order
in returning what we owe.
I remember what someone told me
of a woman whose husband took her ashes,
as she'd asked him to, and with their children
travelled for a year to scatter them
all over the world, a gesture
that tries to say what death allows
in each of us, no matter how we meet it.

It makes me want
to tell you everything:
what I ate for breakfast,
my son's French teacher's name,
how my basil's doing this year
or the deal I got on this Lincoln rocker
from an antique place I've just discovered
on the Wilmer Road. The man there – you'd like
him, Pat – who told me how he'd farmed
for years and years and then risked everything
on something else he loved,
his hands stroking a desk or chair
just as they've bumped the right curve
of a cow's belly, learning the season
of the calf within, listening to wood now,

what to bring forth
from layers of decisions made by strangers,
for their own good reasons.

Remember that day you taught me
how to look for four-leaf clovers?
"Don't try so hard," you kept saying,
"just peek from the corner of your eye,
like this," running your fingers
through a patch and coming up with one
every time, surprised as I was
and with no more faith, but opening
your hand out anyway, that gesture
which belongs to any gamble,
no matter how crazy, the movement
by which a life gets changed
for keeps, a reach
for what we only hope
is there

just as this yearly journey reaches
deeper into what I only thought
I understood: your death
is final, and touching that
brings out the colours – certain
as the grain in oak or cherry –
of a wider life that grows
through the small demands the present makes
pushing me back to the car for the ride home,
already planning the sandwich I'll get
at the truck stop on the highway; empty now,
the woman who runs it taking the time
to put her feet up, sink back
into the knowledge that will hold her
until I arrive; my wave, her smile
what we'll begin with, the common
courtesies, as if they were nothing
to be surprised by.

Bones

INTERVALS

I. Entry

Enough people tell you how comfortable it is
and you come to believe it,
this city opening up
like the map it hands out to tourists,
the parks and the reasonably priced restaurants
enclosed in circles, innocent and reassuring
as the arrows leading you back out to the 401,
the songs on the radio tracing
the same old terrain, love's body
where the prince and the princess live
happily ever after.
Your own childhood. A small girl
eating her spinach out of duty
to the starving, those ragged figures
who still lurk at the edges of polite conversation
like the cities they inhabit, the televised names,
the pictures where women walk through markets
full of soldiers, and kids play
near a parked car, where anything
can happen any minute; though when it does
there's always someone there
between you and the damage, a voice
over the shots of bodies, letting you look
up from the screen
to the square of street outside,
and back to the weather
which will be fine, tomorrow rising
as it always has, with those
who are never asked.

All that talk, what was it
but a need for safety, your life
running on automatic

for as long as you let it,
right up to that night (exactly like any other,
you think now, exactly) when a neighbor
knocked on your door, some figure
from a backyard painting of blue arms,
white squares on a clothesline
suddenly there, a woman, coming to you
her face full of blood, the night
spilling out from her hair
to the street, the man, light glinting
off the metal in his hand
as you pulled her inside.

Where that night's taken you since.
This city, an edge like any other;
its dark, the border territory between houses
where violence holes up in men's hands, the shadows
that fall between a woman's breasts, the kids born
already knowing. Like time bombs, all those childhoods
huddled in corners, these houses
wired to the world, the hum you hear
when you pass, the TV's blue light
spreading into the street and inside
the people, frozen by it,
just sitting there,
waiting.

II. Free Speech

This is for Sylvia
who is deaf
and whose teeth are rotted to the gumline,
stumps in the foul swamp of her mouth
where the noises she makes at us
only her children can understand.
The oldest, fourteen, is smaller
than an eight-year-old, his wrists

thin as the pencil he's using
to mark off the days
their father left them alone, locked
in their cabin forty miles north of here.
Ten, maybe – the pencil hesitates –
no, twelve, with a bag of flour
and a box of powdered milk,
before the cops broke the door down.
This is for him too, for Steven,
round-shouldered old man of a kid,
one hand on the paper, the other
in the air, signing to his mother
the little he has to comfort her
in any language.

Interval House.

Interval: originally
from the Latin inter vallum,
the space between ramparts,
walls, between two events,
two parts of an action, a period
of cessation, a pause

This is for Ruth,
brought in by the police
from Hotel Dieu emergency
eyes swollen shut, broken jaw wired
and eighteen stitches closing one ear. This
is what a man might do
if his wife talked during the 6 o'clock news.
"And I knew better," she tells us softly,
"I guess I just forgot myself."
Tomorrow she may go back to him
("He didn't mean it, he's a good man
really"), but tonight she sits up with me
drinking coffee through a straw.

"I can't sleep," she apologizes,
"every time I close my eyes,
I see his fist coming at me
through the wall."

A house that can accommodate
20 *according to regulations,*
30 *in a pinch, since we don't*
turn anyone away, 32
if we use the old couch
in the back office, maybe 35
if most of them are children
which they are

For Marilyn, aged 7,
her arm crushed because she caught it
in a wringer washer, where she was left,
alone like that, for three days.

Between any fits or periods of disease
an open space lying
between two things
or two periods of one thing

This is for all the time
it's taken me to learn
that terror is not always
sudden, as I thought it was,
the fist or the bomb
ripping the sky open;
that often it is slow
and duller
as August stupefies a city,
that glazed season we come to
out of helplessness,
the wound shut off
from the eye, from the brain

going on, going on alone
behind sheets and sheets of anaesthetic.

The distance between persons
in respect of position, beliefs, etc.
or between things in respect of their qualities,
the difference of pitch between two
musical sounds, an opening

a gap

a 24-hour crisis line

this is for the voices
on the other end I never see,
for all they have time to tell me
before something stops them.

III. ECU*: On the Job*

If I were to place my hand on the side
of her head, the bruise at her left temple
would exactly fit the palm, the heel
curving over her left eye, where the rim
of the heel of her husband's shoe has left
a gash marked out by the doctor's stitches,
which I follow now
applying this ointment to the dry, stretched
and healing skin, beneath which there is only
a thin plate of bone between them
and her brain, where everything happens at once:
the sting of my touch and the ringing of the telephone,
someone laughing in the kitchen
where the dishes are being done, the work
of her lungs as they empty
and fill themselves, the noise
her children are making upstairs

and what will happen to them now;
the brain is adding hydro to food
to first and last month's rent, phone bills
and cough medicine, trying to make ends meet
while it keeps the heart
pumping the blood to her wound,
food for the new cells,
pushing her slowly into the future,
the bruise already yellowing at its edges,
though her husband's still there,
flung into her life again,
nothing left between them but the days
exactly alike, each one bought
at the same cost, and that too
the brain is trying to calculate, a numbness
deep in its centre somewhere
which keeps her eyes turned from mine;
so that for now, her bruise
is the only currency between us.
I carry it home like a paycheque,
my fingers smelling of ointment and blood,
and when someone asks me how it went today
it is the bruise that spills from my mouth,
uncontrolled, incurable, it stains my son's cheek
and grows in secret on my breasts and thighs,
shoots from my husband's knuckles
as he sits there, quietly peeling an orange,
becomes the dark between us in the bed at night.
And maybe it can't be helped.
Maybe it's only what any job
on this planet makes of us,
the shoulders rounded over fifty years
at a sewing machine or a desk, the lungs webbed
with black dust, the cells of a foetus
altered by an eight-hour shift at a computer terminal
day after day. How we've made it seem normal,
when I open the door at 3 a.m.

and the cops are there with another one,
three kids in pyjamas, a few clothes
in a green garbage bag, how this
is just part of their night's work,
as the blood on her cheekbone there
is mine, our daily bread bought with it,
all that we're capable of
and all we can be made to endure,
until even the smallest of us, the babies
I see each day, flinch
when I try to pick them up;
so that that gesture, that grotesque
twisting from another's touch
embodies a future
which includes us all, exactly
as the child growing in the salty fluid of the uterus
includes everything our cells remember
of the long swim in from the sea.

Our future. Though it may be no more
than the last few years of this century
already so full of horrors
that perhaps it can't be helped,
this bruise, no bigger
than the palm of my hand
and beneath it, a woman's brain
still urging her forward.

Something as small as that.
The time we have left
to see it.

IV. Short Story

This isn't one to be told
in the third person,
though we keep on trying to.

My friend describes what happens
with the couple upstairs in her building
and it's like an old movie, only
just the soundtrack, no picture
of the man whose footsteps fill the hallway
outside her bedroom, fade
to a muffled clumping on the stairs
and return with a bang
when the door comes open
over her bed.
Then the thin, unsteady rise
of a woman's anger, and a man's
trying to make her
keep it down. What happens next
could come from westerns or The Three Stooges,
all the slaps and punches, sharp
and exaggerated, the high-pitched clatter
of chairs, but when it falls
from her own ceiling
it's as if she's never heard it before
like the softer thud that blossoms, finally,
in the darkness nearest to her face.
Like any of us, she's frightened
by what she doesn't know
and she tries to explain it
somehow. By the bottles that come out
with their garbage every week
or the dirty children
clogging the front porch.
"Or maybe that's how those people
want to live," she tells me,
as if they choose a life
like a slice of bread, cut clean
from the loaf and eaten with honey
in a warm kitchen.

As if.

So a four-year-old stands in a doorway
yelling at his mother. "Cunt," he screams,
"cunt face! Nothin' but a fuckin' cunt face!"
his words, like the life he's been given, a genetic code
forcing him forward, a blunt weapon,
forcing the story on that way
(this story about *them*, about *those people*)
so that we who hear it can forget
how little is ever really possible
for any of us, botched
failed things to whom it may only come once
and never clearly, that moment
when the voice that tries to sing
through all our stories rises, briefly,
first person singular,
cries *yes* and *now* and *help*
help me.

V. Departure

Always the same beginning:
words and the cells that make them
all that will carry us
into the future.
"I want to get in touch with my feelings,"
a friend says, as if they lived elsewhere,
as if there were more than this, our real selves
different from what we make of each other,
what we accept: these houses
where language capitulates and love
is something to be beaten
out of another's body
or in. *Am I getting through?*
we say to whoever we think
is in there, inside the body
which isn't it,
is a dirty word, allowing everything

that's done, violence taken in
like oxygen becomes the skin
we wear, the atmosphere the planet
turns through, its orbit shrunk
to the will of those
for whom our bodies
are obstacles and nothing more.

In Argentina, a group of scientists
sifts through the mass graves
the death squads planted
cataloguing scattered bones and teeth.
In five months, they make ten
"positive identifications" as they call them.
Ten names. Their eye sockets and jawbones,
their knuckles filled in, their bodies
making room for themselves
out of the numbers this century rushes through,
white noise.

We are that close.

Each of us, who are only
the work of our lungs as they empty
and fill themselves,
the back, the arms
the cells' need, the brain
where all this happens all the time.
All of it and only that.

We are that close.
The time we have left
to do it.

NEIGHBOURS

for Lorna Crozier, who asked

Though don't think you're the only one.
Everybody does.

"So you're from Kingston. The prison town. Well,
what's it like down there, with all those
criminals?"

Sometimes I tell them
Clifford Olson is my next-door neighbour,
he and the other rapists and baby-killers,
their lives down to a few square feet,
a narrow hour in the exercise yard
a block from here at Kingston Pen.

Sometimes I describe
the time I went to P4W
to teach a writing class
where the first woman I met
with her red hair in rollers, a red flowered
housecoat on and those slippers with the pom-poms
also red, red toenails and fingernails,
looked like everybody's aunt from the Big City
who is always more interesting than your mother,
though the truth is she'd chopped her husband up
with an axe.

Another way to answer your question
is to talk about the geology, history
and architecture of this city, built on rock
and out of it; about whether limestone
just naturally piles itself into forts
and prisons, churches, universities, mansions
for the rich or whether the people who settled

couldn't see anything else in it
but their need to wall something in
or out. I could introduce you
to the man whose backyard touches mine.
A retired guard, he'll tell you
things are worse than ever, prisons
run like luxury hotels by asshole politicians,
con-lovers, like the lawyers and social workers
who've never seen the ranges where the guards work;
how can they know? Somebody knifes you
and they act like it's your fault
for being a screw in the first place.
He stuck it out for the pay and the pension,
this house, university for his kids. Not bad
for a guy who never finished high school,
though now he's got this lung disease
and the doctor says it doesn't look good.
Stooped on the back porch, grey and wheezing,
he coughs up forty years of smoke and anger.

A while ago, someone
broke into a friend's house
and beat her unconscious.
For no reason. She came up
from a deep sleep and he was already
there, his hands at her throat.
The police were amazed
when she came to. They showed her
pictures and pictures of young white males.
Is this him? Is this him?
More amazing, she refused to testify,
though all she'll say is that she doesn't feel
prisons are the answer. Her face, when she speaks,
is calm, repaired now, though I think I can see
ragged places in the darks of her
eyes that he tore there, for good.

Some days, when the cries of other victims
rise from the headlines,
I think what she says
is the biggest pile of crap
I've ever had to listen to.
Others, I hear in it
the sound that flows through those who've come back
from a few hours' dying, a current that runs
beneath their descriptions of white light
and someone there to guide you into it,
a parent or a friend, someone from before.

This is when I remember
how the layers of limestone match
the fluctuations of an ancient ocean,
just as the fields outside the city
ride the wider movements
of the rocks that formed the continent.
I remember how the streets here
follow the meeting of lake and river
so that you never end up
where you think you're going to.

Some days, when the guy at the back
comes out to say hello, his look
is the one my dad's face had
after his heart attack, that big man
suddenly lying there, staring up at us
for the first time, embarrassed to suffer
what so many others have already had to.
In his grey face, something opens,
softly. Like those colours
that tint the skin of limestone
when you really look at it.
Some days, I drive home
through fields July's brought little to
but the common yellows of hawkweed, mustard;

colours, I read somewhere, that insects see
as ultraviolet, a luminescent landscape
we can't use, though the city
rises from it, scared and hopeful,
like a friend I haven't seen in years
who wants to show me in her walk
or how she's done her hair
another way of wearing
everything I thought I'd recognize.

CHANGE OF HEART

Ford Madox Ford taught that you couldn't have a man appear long enough to sell a newspaper in a story unless you put him there with enough detail to make the reader see him.
– Flannery O'Connor in "Writing Short Stories"

It was my aunt who taught me
how to pick the last tomatoes
when they were still green
and wrap them in newspaper,
store them away in the dark
where they'd ripen on their own,
surprising me with their colour
long after the red was gone
from the trees, the dried leaves banked
around the sage and the oregano.

I still don't know how they did it,
there, without the sun.
Or why I want
to let them surface here
when I'm trying to write
about a change of heart,
as if some homely metaphor
about it growing sweeter,
like a piece of fruit,
is going to make it easier
to tell you
it belongs to the man in the last poem,
the man you saw long enough
for him to beat my friend unconscious.
You're no Pollyanna. You know
the real thing, the warning
your own heart gives out
when you're alone, at night, crossing
the parking lot to your car, knowing

the guy's still out there.
It's me who needs to put him
here, describe the night it hit home:
this was it, his one and only life,
the days that followed, documented evidence
of a changing heart, maybe some AA meetings
or an upgrading course at the high school,
the job he's held for three years now,
his wife and their new baby.
I'd like to make it
his voice, coming to you
as the one witness you can trust,
but instead, there's only mine.

I have a friend with fair hair
and a way with children.
One night a man broke
into her house and beat her up.
She survived and after the bruises
finished with her, she got up
and went back to work. As she does
every day now, waking every morning
to that silence which surrounds
her life, in which she must decide
again, and for today only,
how she will live with the memory
of his fists. And I tell you
my need to believe this
is the closest I will ever come
to faith, that atmosphere
in which no one I know
can live, very long, any more.
Me, here, trying to survive it
long enough to make you see
how my friend, who decides
each morning, also remembers
as I believe the man who beat her

remembers her screams, and each day
has to make from them
a way of speaking to the muscles
that control his hands, to the stammer
he thinks of as his changed heart,
and to the finer chemistries
that make up, and renew him,
every seven years, exactly
as he is, affirming everything.

BURN-OUT

is what happens
when you work too hard
in one of the *caring professions*
as they're called these days.
It has definite symptoms
and most workplaces now
offer seminars to discuss it,
distribute burn-out pamphlets
in the staff room.

For me, though,
it's my old apartment on West Street,
after the fireman turned to where
I was standing on the sidewalk
and said "OK, we'll take you in now
for a minute." How the place was
colder than I'd thought possible,
the broken windows, the walls
smeared with soot and the wet
grit under my feet. And the smell,
the smell I couldn't get out
of even the few things
I wanted to try to save.

Beyond that, it's the door
to the staff office, Interval House,
a shelter for battered women and children.
I'm sitting in there now,
the walls around me plastered
with kids' drawings, notices, telephone messages
and photographs, at a desk littered with coffee mugs
and matchbooks, ashtrays, a telephone
and the book you record the calls in, a soother,
pens, a bottle of shampoo, some cough drops,
a kid's mitten and two pairs of earrings. It is

8:30 p.m. and I am only
four hours in
to a twelve-hour shift.

I wish I could tell you
that the kids are all in bed,
the women getting ready
to watch a movie on TV,
someone making popcorn in the kitchen.
I wish I could lay in a music track,
as I could if this were a film,
so that you'd catch snatches
of Holly Near, maybe, or Joni Mitchell,
yes, even my tinny, six-year-old voice
way back there in Sunday School, singing
Jesus bids us shine with a clear,
pure light because, damn it, that's
here too, but not tonight.
Tonight,
I have eight more hours to go
when Linda comes in, shuts
the door, lights a cigarette.
Her face has that look
I've learned to recognize
but tonight, all I know
is that it's just my luck
to have to be here, watching
as her mouth forces the words
out from some hidden place
so far within her she might
never have found them, never,
into this room, where they become
a job I'm not quite
up to, not tonight "… it wasn't
alive, I mean, but it was
something, you know, I was maybe
five months along, and afterwards

he got a kitchen knife to cut the,
you know, the cord and put
it in a garbage bag, he
wouldn't let me go to the
hospital and that was a year ago,
I never told anybody, but
I have to
now."

And again, I wish I could tell you
how I handled this in a
professional manner, except that
I, personally, don't think there
is one. Professional always makes me think
of when I was at school
and the teacher told us
there was no such word
as the word "can't."
"You *can* do it! You *can*,"
my gym teacher screams at me
as I gather for a broad jump, leap
into some weakness in the joint
a grandmother'd left me. For good.
An accident it's called,
that juncture between
what happens to you
and what you have
to meet it with,
which isn't always enough.

So Linda and I
just sit here. She's crying,
but for a minute more, I still hear
the doctor, standing over me
shaking his head, talking of
"... *chondromalacia* ... *osteoarthritis* ...
due to repeated injury, which

always burns itself out, so that
the joints, though stiff of course,
are ultimately painless,"
and I reach
for my knee (cradling it
as I might a child's head
sleeping, in my lap) as I will
in the next movement, reach
for Linda's shoulder
in that gesture which,
from where you are, may appear
ambiguous, whether it's for
comfort or support, though
believe me, it's not
the distance makes it
seem that way, it's not
the distance, at all.

BONES

for Barb

A story of yours got this one going,
so I'm sending it back now, changed of course,
just as each person I love
is a relocation, where I take up
a different place in the world.

The way you told it, it was after midnight,
you coming off the late shift, heading home
in a taxi, a woman driving,
and you ask her if she's ever scared
working these hours and she says, "No, I've got this
to protect me!" reaching under her seat
to pull up (you expected a crowbar,
a tire iron) this eight-inch, stainless steel
shank. "The pin from my mother's thigh,"
she tells you, "I got it when they put
one of those new plastic ones in."

Sometimes when I tell myself this story
I get caught up in logistics,
how the doctor must have delivered the thing
from layers of fat and muscle
into one of those shiny dishes
the nurse is always holding
and then she would have,
what? washed it off? wrapped it in towels?
carried it down to the waiting room, the daughter
sitting there, reading magazines, smoking cigarettes?
It's so improbable, like the foetus
pickled in a jar in the science lab in high school,
though other times it's just
there, natural as the light
that bounces off it,

somebody's mother's thigh bone,
for protection, like her face
in the hall light, rescuing you
from a nightmare.

You told me this
during my visit last year
when I'd just quit working
at the crisis centre, that job
that wrenched me round
until each morning stretched, a pale, dry skin,
over the real colour of the day,
ready to spring at me, like the child
whose hand had been held down
on a red-hot burner
reappearing in the face of a woman
met casually at a cocktail party.
Everywhere I went, my work experience
drew me through confessions I couldn't stop,
and I couldn't stop talking about them
so you had to listen
but, being you, in that way that listening
can be active, when the listener re-enters
the country of her own damage
from a new direction.

This can be like watching someone we love
return from the limits a body can be taken to
– a botched suicide, say, or an accident.
Years, it might be, before the eyes or the hands retrieve enough
to offer as a sign,
what doctors think they can detect
on a CAT scan, some pattern in the cells
to show them, once and for all,
how the mind, like the body, makes shape
of what's left, the terrible knowledge
it labours through, slowly regaining itself.

Though on an X-ray, even the bones show up
as light, a translucence that belies their strength
or renders it immeasurable,
like the distances we count on them to carry us,
right to the end of our lives and back again,
and again.

Nearer to Prayers Than Stories

KOKO

Hands developed with terrible labor by apes
Hang from the sleeves of evangelists …
– Robert Bly in "The Great Society"

Only now it is our terrible labour
(or what we thought was ours, alone)
unfurling from the root-black fingers
of an ape. Koko, the talking gorilla.
In Ameslan, her hands are muscular
and vibrant as vocal cords, name
colours and distinguish *had* and *will*,
can make a metaphor; they choose
a tailless kitten for a pet
and christen him *All-Ball*, lie
when they need to and insult their trainer
Penny dirty toilet devil, a repertoire
of over 500 words that upset
Descartes, Marx, our known,
human world. Not to mention fellow linguists
who say it's all a trick – Polly, Polly
pretty bird or Mr Ed. They point
to her IQ score, a meagre 85,
though when they asked if she'd choose
a tree or a house for shelter
from the rain, she chose a tree
and got marked wrong.

Who says
and what
is what it comes to, though,
the sky filling up with satellites,
the cities with paper, whole stores
of greeting cards for everything
we can't spit out ourselves,
like the scratch at the back of the brain
we no longer recognize as memory.

On the TV Reagan and Gorbachev in Geneva,
though their names don't matter much,
just two more faces over shirts and ties
discussing missile size, the "nitty-gritty"
as a spokesman puts it, while
"women are more interested in peace
and things of that nature …
the human interest stuff."

The human interest.
Kinda like the swings in the park
across from here, how they always
squeak, day in, day out.
The guys who trim the grass
and keep the benches painted
don't even try to fix them anymore;
they know some things are like that,
stubborn as hell, no matter how much
you make an hour or what kind of government
you get. So that what we have are humans
in Oslo, Leningrad, Peking, Thunder Bay,
Denver, Córdoba and Rome pushing their kids
on swings that *squeak*   *squeak*   *squeak*
like the creaks
and farts and stutterings the body makes
to say *here* and *here* and *here.*

After living with them,
Jane Goodall found that chimpanzees
use tools, which leaves us language
as the last thing
we've got, we think,
and at the compound, Koko looking out,
a reporter tries to keep it:

"Are you an animal or a person?"

The hands coming up, almost
before he's done: *Fine animal gorilla.*
Close to the chest, showing him
familiar palm and fingers
sing *fine* caress *animal.*

SEEING IS BELIEVING

for Kathie

You tell me you believe in magic
and at first I'm with you, fitting
your words to my own vision: how hard work's
made these paws of ours subtle enough
to pull a rabbit from a hat
or rescue Venus from a hunk of rock.
But then I see you mean it
literally, that look in your eye
the warning light at which my mind
brakes and switches to reverse
like the flashing orange note I can hear
at any distance when someone starts up
about intense religious experiences;
"... they talk of hallowed things, aloud,
and embarrass my dog," said Emily Dickinson
and I agree, stiffened in my chair
while you trace, with thin
quick hands and endless cigarettes,
a fourth, fifth, eighth dimension
from which birds and wolves
appear at will, worlds
we can travel to ourselves,
"as we used to," you say, "by flying
outside our bodies!"

Outside your windows,
your prairie winter stretches
further than I can, Kathie,
my imagination bumbling
like a fly awakened in the wrong season
against these tiny squares
that open onto so much sky.
And from the tapedeck, a song of Ferron's

fills the space this side with her
brand of longing – *I am looking for something*
outside of forgiveness – the last notes
following the smoke from your cigarette
into the light you're silhouetted by, the white
of the next field stunning my eyes
as they find someone else out there
moving alone and steadily into it.

I want to cry out to them
"Be careful! Be careful!" but I know
it's me I'm really talking to.
Just like the other day
when we were driving into Calgary,
all that white, that sky again,
and I wanted to ask you, "Kathie,
are you here for good?"
as if I could make your choice
a question still, after fifteen years.
I remember the road coming
to a slight rise then; there was this
white house, a barn and a few
scraggly trees that you slowed for,
"Look," you said, "I love that place,
it's so much like Ontario," laughing
at my shriek of denial, but sticking
to what you'd said, both of us right,
just as a woman can see
why her friends can't understand
what she sees in some guy
and go on seeing it
at the same time.

So, Kathie, you've brought me to this notion
that the place we end up in
goes deeper than choice, if we're lucky.
Do you know what I mean? How a friend

in Toronto suffers from allergies
that clear up
the day she moves to the west coast
while someone else writes
to his family in St John's
from Australia, saying "I'm home at last!"
I never was to Africa, Ferron's singing,
but it comes up in my dreams
and though we'll never be able to chart it, probably,
it's in our blood, what geneticists will come to
in a lab someday, some ancestor's love
for a climate or a skyline
reaching out to plant us
in the place where we'll do best.

I'd even call it scientific,
though I know you'd hate
the word, want to soften
the borderlines between my brand
of magic and your own: all those countries
where we range, halfway between hope and theory.
Just as I imagine you some days,
driving, driving, your need
mapped by wind and that sky
always moving, always reaching
to that point on the horizon
where limitation and possibility
seem to come to the same thing,
while I write this in Ontario,
February, that month when grey and white
is all I see, but see it
as I hear the sound that grows
in Eastern prayer chants,
African drumming, from the way
a single note is played
a little differently each time, until the music
fills these fields, whose movement

to the time it takes
to wear a mountain down
sets even the oldest landmark drifting.

NIGHTWORK

Every day is thought upon and calculated, but the night is not premeditated.
– Matthew O'Connor, in Djuna Barnes's Nightwood

I always wanted to be the one
who drove the snowplough, me
and a tall red thermos, like the one
my dad took into the plant, high up
in the cab, driving through it. Could see
the sun, rising on the arc
the wipers made, like the waves
from the neighbours, sleepy and bundled,
digging their cars out as I passed.
And then it was flour
I wanted to plough through, mounds of it
falling around me in a bakery,
the round loaves rising;
and after that, the white uniforms
of nurses, cool as their hands
pulling someone up from a fever dream,
from the middle of the night.

Later, of course, I read Marx
and learned that bakers in the 1860s
died in their thirties, exhausted
from their eighteen-hour shifts, children crushed
in the rolling mills where they'd fallen
asleep, after twelve hours. Later,
I learned for myself, that year
in the parts plant how the days
fall in on themselves, as they did
when my son was small,
when my grey need for sleep
drifted like cobwebs
through my brain cells.

And yet, even then, I remember
standing by the window, his hot
damp cheek on my shoulder, looking out
over the city to the lights of the supermarket
where someone was piling the shelves
high with cans of peaches, opening some
to share at coffee break
with the guys from the meat department
who'd grilled a couple of steaks,
maybe fried some onions and mushrooms,
one of the ways they'd found
to cut the losses the job left
in the only time they had, like the calls
that office cleaners make to relatives
in England or India, "all over the world,"
one of them told me once, "a whole life
we build up for ourselves, from the big
fat desks of IBM executives."
And I remember the night I was in labour
with my son, when the doctor arrived
in a tuxedo, looking worried. It was
his anniversary and they'd just sat down in
a fancy restaurant, to champagne,
when his pager beeped. "Get me out of here
by nine," he laughed, "and I'll buy you
a bottle of Mumm's." I did my best,
though it was hard to imagine him
with another life outside of
this one; "Open your eyes,"
Ron whispered, as I hunched,
pushing, and I saw my son's
opening into mine
as his head emerged
as his shoulders slid forward
as he was lifted to my stomach
where he turned toward me, as any
animal will, smelling sex or food.

Later he took my breast, that first tug
travelling to my fingertips, the narrowest
pocket of my lungs, each fold of brain
or intestine, every crease
in the soles of my feet,
like light coming on
in a room I'd only half-inhabited
to show me for the first time
exactly where I was, how I belonged
to the laughter of the nurses
as they changed shift, and to that
of the doctor and his wife, dancing,
Fred and Ginger, among waiters, musicians,
chandeliers, women with jewels in their hair,
Ron's kiss, as he left, the snow
just starting in the streets outside, the tracks
of his tires from the hospital parking lot
to the one at Harvey's, cheeseburger and shake
handed out to him by someone pimply and heavy-eyed,
the skid into our driveway, last night's paper
stuck in the door, the telephone operator
awake, ready to place his call, bringing
my mother to the news she'd waited for, for years,
my mother, standing in the kitchen, calling
Air Canada, VIA, my father putting
the coffee on, the man who drives
the snowplough, starting up.

THINGS

My first car was a blue Volkswagen beetle
Mike Longmoore built for me
out of the old parts that sprouted in his backyard
overnight, like mushrooms;
and something that car took in
(maybe from the rain or the cryptic soil)
gave it an organic personality.
I'm not saying it was anything like a human,
or even another animal we'd recognize,
just that it was a car you didn't *drive,* really.
Instead you had to think of *going places together,*
and only those who understood this perfectly
could get it to start in the first place.
Of course, I talked to it; clumsily at first
just as you learn to converse with your dog
or your maidenhair fern, but gradually
I got the hang of it, though I wasn't there
the day my brother took it to the beer store
and the big green Pontiac with the drunken salesman
came through the stop sign; so I can only imagine
that moment, between impact and shudder,
when it realized it was only metal after all.

Of course, that car's not the only thing.
A pair of green shorts I had
when I was fourteen, the exact shade
and texture of summer. Or a salad bowl
I've seasoned so often, we wear each other's smell
as lovers do, another kind of skin.
A rag doll my brother brought me
from an Indian woman in the mountains of the Yucatan,
herself in miniature, wearing her clothes,
her eyes and nose stitched in with yarn,
and below that, where the mouth should be,

a blank she'd left
to tell of the silences between women.

What is it for you? The thing you love
for the beauty of it, heft
of a well-turned bowl or the singing precision
of a sharp knife, how the foot feels
against the spade that slides willingly
into the earth, tables that make
the mouth water, chairs without spiritual pretensions
who know that their duty is to the body
in all its moods, the carved walnut box
for keeping secrets in,
all the hockey sticks, axe handles,
canoe paddles, tennis rackets, boomerangs
that come to you
from those who use wood
to tell what they know of movement,
all the things we make
to nourish the body and its life,
whatever takes its purpose
from our limitations
and seeks to bless them
even in small ways.
That is our history here
though we had to get out of the trees to make it.
Before that, everything we share
with the chimpanzees, hanging around
picking nits off each other.

Now it's things that connect us.
They are social beings after all,
leading complex, cosmopolitan lives.
The woman who cuts my hair has these scissors
she spent hundreds on. They're worth
every penny too because they
understand so perfectly

whatever her fingers tell them
even though she has to send them to Japan
once a year to be sharpened.
"Because only the person who made them
can do it properly," she tells me,
"it's the way things are." She's right, of course,
and there are hundreds of scissors like hers
all over the world. I can hear the clatter
their stiletto blades make in the airports,
their round eyes cutting through clouds
as the plane descends into Tokyo.
And as for the plane, what is it
but a thing we've made to carry
other things? And ourselves, too, but only
to buy and sell things, find out
how other people make them, trade them,
take pictures of them, staring at the ones
that live in museums and art galleries,
scrounging the earth for those still
caught in it, left behind by the dead,
their lives frozen in them
as blown glass holds the glass-maker's breath.

Once the Neanderthals had tools
they dug graves where archaeologists
can find the dust of flowers
someone placed beside the body.
For a purpose, which still
reaches out, palpable,
ambiguous as a word
or the hundreds of gestures we've made
to say *yes* or *no*.
That coffee mug you hold each morning
without even thinking about it
is a mystery. Reveals what our need makes
from sand and heat, what it trusts
to cardboard boxes, straw, metal staples,

asphalt, diesel fuel and the oily roar
of jet planes. Is a lifetime
on the road or in a factory,
the fifteen-minute break the guy
who loaded the plane is taking
at the edge of the runway before he loads
the socket wrenches for a bike shop in Utah,
a Coke in one hand, a cigarette
stinging his lips. A greeting,
borrowed from the earth to bring comfort,
holds us.

STUNTS

(a poem inspired by The Guinness Book of World Records *and an interview with Philippe Petit in* People *magazine)*

The ones they can't pull off
bring us nothing. Houdini's dying promise
to return. How he must have climbed into his death
with the simple faith he'd demonstrated
all his life: if there's a way in,
there's a way out. Counting on us
to believe it this time too, forgetting
the fist in his gut, the abrupt fall
into what it made of him.

Forgetting his body like that, though the trick's
there or nowhere, doing it over and over again
until it comes, another way of talking.
What the high-wire artist means
when he says that running is the acrobat's laughter.
"When my heart is open to the wind," he tells us,
"I am next to the gates of Paradise. Our domain
is bounded by death, not props."
And we can see how he holds to that,
the balance pole that gives him
the patience of one who has fallen before
and believes he will get
what he deserves.

As we all want to.
So that when Annie Edson Taylor,
first person down Niagara Falls in a barrel,
climbed out and said, "Nobody ought ever
to do that again," nobody listened.
It wasn't her advice
that got her over, any more than it's the air
that keeps the divers from the rocks

at La Quebrada or the roar of the cannon
that Zacchini flies with, at 54 m.p.h.
When the wind cuts through our overcoats
as we walk home from work, we know
Petit feels it too
as he steps out between the towers
of the World Trade Center,
1350 feet above our heads;
and as our fingers fumble for our keys
we are glad for the ones
that keep a yo-yo going, 5 days
non-stop, or write the Lord's Prayer
34 times on a postage stamp.
We know what they look like,
no further escaped from a fin or a claw
than our own; so that it pleases us,
when the day boils up
smelling of burnt milk, when we're out of coffee
and the egg runs down our chins,
to know that someone's out there, for us,
making omelettes while dangling from a helicopter,
catching a grape in their mouth at 319 feet
or climbing a 30-foot coconut tree
in 4.88 seconds, barefoot.
To know we're deserving sometimes,
as Petit steps out
into that instant, bounded by air
at the edge of the crowd's hope,
where everything comes easy
and the body fits.

ORDINARY MOVING

From here, I see my son round the corner
on his skateboard, heading home,
knees slightly bent to steer the thing
around parked cars, a wiry dance
in which the body pivots
on the bump of the wheels, while the feet
stay firmly grounded, save for one last move
– after he's turned it up the driveway to a spot
just there – when he jumps off, flips it
with his toe to lean against the back step, ready
for take off, the whole performance
that mixture of nonchalance and theatre
I recognize from the movies, especially the ones
where Bogart shoves a handful of hundreds into his pocket,
uncrumples them later for drinks or the cost
of straightening a girl's club foot, his way
of tipping his hat or lighting a cigarette
filling the screen with his past,
with the present state of the world, even
as clearly as my son fills out
his thirteen summers in a curve
that brings the littler kids
up from their sandboxes, just to watch.

Sometimes a voice can do this too.
That auctioneer I heard last week,
one of the best, I'm told , though my
poor imitation – *iń at eighty-five, whó'll say*
ninety. I've ǵot eighty-five, whó'll say
ninety. Nińety's in, who'll give me ninety-five,
nińety-five, who's gót ninety-five
Nińety's góing, do I hear ninety-five.
Five. Five. Do I hear ninety-five. Soĺd for
nińety dóllars, number one-eight-síx – can't give you
her hands, singing their part, threading

the air between the high, gold line
of a Gibbard sideboard and the grey eyes
of the woman in green, holding out for it.
You'll have to call that up
from yourself; the day, the yard
and what's in it, the house emptied,
saying *now what*   *now what* will all be
yours, just as the childhood
that returns when I chant *Ordinary, moving,*
Laughing, talking can belong to no one else,
though it's right where my voice
enters your brain
that our two childhoods meet.

On the beach, all the people
move through the heat between sand
and sky. Ordinary moving, all this
clumsy flesh, the gawkiness that mumbles
through its cramped litany of pain, getting
on with it, the scars half-hidden under
towels or T-shirts keeping their boasts,
bargains struck against a future
that must wait, a few years more,
to lay its claim. All the people move,
each body wearing more life
than it thought possible at first,
and worn by it too, proof positive
that nothing is ever past. Look,
that man there swings his daughter
to his shoulders, his hands so big
they cover her knees and hold her
up as surely as she and she alone
holds him. In the width of her palm,
or the length of her toes, in whatever
she takes from this hour, from its heat
and the smell of his skin rising through it,
from the sound of his voice,
for later when it's no longer his.

All these people, moving
on this beach of mine. Or yours,
like the auctioneer or the child
on the skateboard in whatever street,
whatever city, even Bogart grinning down
from a million screens, larger than life
and still no bigger than our own, each one
unfolding into another's, almost as easily
as parents come to love their children, those perfect
strangers to whom we surrender everything,
and as abruptly as summer arrives
in my part of the country – for a few
short weeks at best, but as if it were
the only season, ever, all its heat
spilling open
in a single afternoon.

IDYLL

The baby is playing
with an empty potato chip bag.
Or rather, *the* potato chip bag, the one
that dropped from her sister's hand
when she jumped up and ran
back to the other kids
splashing out there, where the sun
hurts her eyes. "Bag," she said,
"play with the bag, Kelly,"
and now the baby knows the crack
and glitter, the metal-salt
vinegar smell, the gritty
taste of the word, a sound
she can grow for hours in
like *milk* or *sleep*.

Behind her, the dog is chewing
on an old bone he's dragged
from under the hedge, his eyes
flicking from the baby to the beach
and back, up to the adults
sitting on lawn chairs, eating hotdogs,
sharing with them this love
of being in the sun, chewing
and watching other animals
(just as, in a recent interview,
a famous film-maker said
he got his ideas from shopping centres,
walking around with his walkman on,
eating ice-cream and staring).

For almost an hour the eight-year-old's
been trying to stand upright
on the inner tube, if only for a minute,
so that by now she knows

the stretch and tighten of calf and thigh,
the tremor her toes cling to
at one foot up, the slithering dip
of half-crouch to the sleek
whoosh slip beneath both feet
that tips her into a splat of cold.
Above her, she can feel
the sky's patience, gentle
as her mother's is sometimes,
letting her know she can grow
to meet it, just as her brother
on the dock finds how
to draw his afternoon around him
with the flick and curve of wrist and forearm
as he casts and casts
the bright rapala spinning to plop
near a stump or a rock, wanting only
that answering tug, sunfish or rock bass
he doesn't care, though he knows the story
of the big one down there, older,
his grandfather says, than the cottage,
feels it nibble at the base of his brain
while another part of his mind
swims back and forth,
trying to decide about noise
whether the younger kids
splashing behind him
bring the fish or scare them,
how some people say
you have to keep perfectly still,
yet Charlie Saunders catches more
than anyone, banging his frying pans
over the side of the boat
before he casts, "to get 'em
mad," he says and the boy plans
to try it, though he also knows
that "getting a fish mad" is an

anthropomorphism, the word his dad gave him
surfacing with a smile as he brings the rapala in,
looks at it, decides to try worms.

And all the time, the adults
keep on talking. Nothing stops them.
Though a question has to loop
and swim around a sand castle,
someone wading out too far, a toddler
reaching for a cracker, skinned elbows
and the need for more beer,
it makes its way at last
to bring the answer back.
Everyone laughs and the day
remembers itself, drifts on.
Someone starts to think about
taking the chicken out of the fridge,
maybe shelling some peas, when dark
against the far shore, a girl teeters
yelling "Mommy, Daddy!" a fish
flashes to the dock in a spray of light,
the dog jumps up, barking, someone
swings the baby to a hip, yelling
"Look at that!" and the crumpled bag skims
over the grass, eddies in the shade there
where the sun's hit the beech trees.

LIFELINES

Like no one before
He let out a roar
And I just had to tag along
Each night I went to bed
With the sound in my head
And the dream was a song.
– from John Fogerty's "Big Train (from Memphis)"

Now I'm no singer, so I used to think
I'd only come to music from the back door,
the sidelines, like I came to baseball
or motorcycles, always the passenger,
which was fine in its way, how Elvis
got me started, loud
as he could go on my green portable,
my father downstairs yelling
SHUT THAT DAMN THING OFF
ignored, as he had to be.
Like the night Elvis was on Ed Sullivan
– if only from the waist up –
and my mother's hands went
to her mouth, confirming
what I knew
about what I needed.

How I could ride
flat out like that, one voice
for a mood or a season,
years of Dylan when everyone I knew
or ever would know
seemed to be on the road
angry and sure of our destination
even if it meant just not going back.
Songs that opened into rooms,
the place I lived with Peter, "All You Need

Is Love" and "Brown-Eyed Girl," like the smoke
and the red wine that carried us
into the long, long nights; I could go on,
but you've got your own lifeline, surely,
humming it now, I'll bet, as you hear this,
confident that it will all come back,
"Teen Angel" on the car-radio the other day
and me singing along, word-perfect,
everyone else suddenly silent
as if I'd just dropped in
from another planet.

Which I had, in a way,
all the brain cells
where I've stored the energy
for just that kind of travelling,
so that now I do thirty years,
easy, in an hour and not just
straight through, either,
detours and double-backs, leaps,
butting the Beatles up against the Talking Heads
or a voice like Ferron's charting
all the places Dylan's never will.

Re-mapping my life, you could say, the way
this poem began, with a song
and something smaller too: one of those styrofoam cups
you get for take-out coffee, Chris and me stopping
for some the other day, and him standing by the car
tearing a little hole in the plastic lid – you know
how you do, so it won't spill – and saying
that every time he does that
he goes right back
to all those dumb jobs, all those summers
on the rail gang or the paving crew, the years
in the paint factory, all the breaks
when he'd stand in the doorway

or the shade of the spreader, just staring,
the cup going cold in his hand.
The shock of it now, feeling
his heart make room again
for the wanting and wanting that cramped it
into the tightest corner of his chest,
that spark in a synapse somewhere
regaining for him
something else he thought he'd given up on,
saying *look, you have time, even yet*
to come to love this too.

My son asks if he's growing
every second and I say yes
knowing he'll go straight on
to bamboo shoots, while I catch
this crazy image of the double helix
spiralling at the centre of each cell,
my layman's view of DNA, bright filaments
of light or sound the body moves to
in the dance it makes through what it's given
what it's trying to become,

just as I dance on a Saturday afternoon
in an empty house, for hours sometimes,
all the selves I am ambiguous
and incomplete, as always,
as the same old rhythms rise
and change and relocate themselves,
keeping it up, keeping on
for as long as I do.

PARTICULARS

To come back, again,
to those Sundays at my grandmother's table,
but by a different way, so that I see
that thin spot in my father's hair
as he bowed his head to ask
the blessing – what my grandmother
called it, not thanks – *Bless*
this food to our use
and us to Thy service,
in Christ's name,
Amen. My father stumbling
over the words, perhaps in recognition
of what he was really asking for
(there, in the midst of things,
his whole family listening),
a blessing, on food they'd earned
casting metal, teaching other people's kids
or planted, themselves, in the fields we'd see
as soon as we raised our heads, men and women
embarrassed by prayer, but sticking to it
as they stuck to their stories,
hoarded those private, irreducible histories
that no one else would get a piece of, ever.

To begin to see, a little,
what they taught me
of themselves, their place
among the living and the dead,
thanksgiving and the practical
particulars of grace, and to accept it,
slowly, almost grudgingly,
to come downstairs this morning
as the paper slaps
the front porch, look up, catch
the paper girl with her walkman on

dancing down the street, red tights,
jean jacket, blonde hair, making me
love her, perfectly, for ten seconds,
long enough to call out
all my other loves, locate each one
precisely, as I could this house
on a city map or the day I found
my son, swimming within me.

To try and hear it
in the way we make the most
of what we get, like the man I know
who says he's held Death in his arms.
That's how he puts it, trying
for a way to say *wife* or *Ellen*
and reach far enough to touch her
there, include the whispers
from the hall outside, the hiss
of the oxygen tank, still on,
the sounds his arms made
adjusting to her weight, this
angle of bone, this one
when her head tipped, finally, back.

And to say for myself, just once,
without embarrassment, *bless,*
thrown out as to some lightness
that I actually believe in,
surprised (as I believe
they were) to find it
here, where it seems impossible
that one life even matters, though
like them, I'll argue
the stubborn argument of the particular,
right now, in the midst of things, *this*
and *this.*

Keep That Candle Burning Bright

... my words are the garment of what I shall never be
Like the tucked sleeve of a one-armed boy.
– *W.S. Merwin, "When You Go Away"*

Keep That Candle Burning Bright: Poems for Emmylou Harris

DEDICATION

These poems are for Emmylou Harris, sparked by a song called "Burn That Candle" which Winfield Scott wrote and she sings on an album called *Quarter Moon in a Ten Cent Town.*

A song that reminds me of the kid who wanted to be a singer, who was me. Who couldn't believe it when the choir teacher said (the Sunday School choir, where they had to take everybody), when she said, *How about you just mouth the words, dear,* and put me in the back row as if it were no big deal.

These poems are for then and for now, too. All those times when I just can't help it and a song bursts through and the people around me contort to poses from the Spanish Inquisition screaming *Stop! Please stop!* – so I don't even sing in the shower anymore, out of respect for the water's perfect pitch, how it sings out onto the tiles.

They are for everything I acquiesce to at weddings and concerts, funerals, those parties where someone picks up a guitar (as – oh! – I've always wanted to) and everyone else joins in, right on key, and I just sit there, mouthing the words. They try to measure that silence which, I know, is immeasurable, is the lifetime's distance between fact and longing which, like all of us, I keep on trying to close.

They remember the songs I've played over and over, the worn spots on a record album, the grooves wearing away to become the convolutions of my brain, singing for everything I couldn't be.

These poems are for Emmylou Harris, to say *thanks for the songs,* for how they sing of hot summer nights on the highway and wine and falling in love and Jesus and the light someone puts in the window to guide you home.

They are homely like that and corny and clichéd.

And necessary, yes, as my love for that kid who still embarrasses me, angers, hurts, the kid who fails.

They burn from what is strong in me, as each of us, in our best moments, tries to love the noisy, untidy selves we've lost, out there somewhere.

That's what I hope, anyway. That she'll know. Know it's me who's calling. My voice like a candle in the night, bringing her in.

WALKIN' SHOES

Another thing I like about Emmylou Harris is how the boots she's wearing on the album cover always fit her songs: sleek and expensive on *Elite Hotel,* fringed and slightly sleazy on *Evangeline,* white with sleek black toes on *White Shoes.* And when she favours pink, it's not just any pink. The boots she's wearing on *Angel Band* are what I think of as old-fashioned, spiritual pink, almost mauve, like those unspectacular, but heavenly-scented roses country gardens used to grow, while the ones on *The Ballad of Sally Rose* shimmer with the surprising incandescence of Bob Dylan's hat when he walks on stage in *The Last Waltz* or that split-second of sunset in early July, if you catch it from a canoe, in the middle of a lake, with a thermos of good coffee beside you.

I know what Freud says about the connection between shoes and vaginas and I say *so what.* Because I am a woman with bad knees and feet that are hard to fit, I know how hard it is for a good shoe to be simply that. When I slide an album back into its jacket and see the perfect fit of song to shoeleather, I remember how my foot feels when that happens, the silkiness and sensuous smell, the supple energy with which this idea of my foot fits my foot itself, a spiritual energy, as when The Word becomes flesh and my life unfolds before me, endless reflections in a three-way mirror, each incarnation inevitable as the new fall line from Italy, letting me know I will be born again as a country singer with great legs.

I know I'll feel better, when I slide down into the leather sings Emmylou when she sings "White Shoes," a song in which she wakes up from a dream and sees them in a magazine and goes out and gets them and wears them out on the town that night and meets The Guy. A song which I now understand to be a religious parable, just like "Wheels" or any of those other songs she sings about truckers, heading Home.

From where I am now, the planet, criss-crossed with roads and trails and paths and streets and sidewalks, is the only map of heaven I can rely on, so I choose my way and start out. In my good shoes, which my feet love and my soul needs, as my spirit needs my lungs, needs the space they have to work in, which the body gives.

SONGBIRDS AND HURTIN' SONGS

Of course, when I'm listening to Emmylou Harris, I'm listening to a whole lot of other people at the same time, like Gram Parsons, Rodney Crowell, Kitty Wells, Chuck Berry, Merle Haggard, Dolly Parton and at least two busloads of church choirs. All that proves is that nobody sings alone, though it's equally true that nobody, not even Emmylou Harris, will ever sing "Sweet Dreams of You" the way Patsy Cline did and that Jesse Winchester's rendition of "Songbird" can't hold a candle to Emmylou's. This is what I mean when I say that all lives weave that way, in and out, between all that we share and all that we don't, manners and mystery, History and the moment I get called on, as you do, to be nobody but me.

And since you already know all that, you'll also know what I mean when I say there's nothing like country for a hurtin' song, something to do with steel strings, I think, and the way a country voice isn't afraid to let you hear the places where it breaks, that twang it gets from carrying bluegrass and gospel a little further west.

A voice like that knows something about how to carry longing, too. I mean the hard, practical work of it, day to day. How Emmylou gets over it just long enough to let her heartache mend and then starts loving him again, her voice filling every note until it cracks and everything she's lost spills over, filling me up with all I have to lose, until I'm clumsy with the weight of it. How it's just that – in the voice – that shows me what I can't find by myself. How it sings on, using its breaking to do it.

DRIVING

I know someone who insists that Emmylou Harris saved her life the year she left her husband. It was all so crazy, the only thing my friend could stand to listen to was *Pieces of the Sky* and now, whenever I hear it, I see her driving, at night, the tape deck blaring, driving on and on.

Sometimes it seems that everyone I know has a story that happens on a highway. My friend Jim likes to tell about the time his car broke down, in a storm, on the 401 and he was so mad he sold the goddamn thing for a dollar to the tow-truck driver, walked the rest of the way to Toronto, not even noticing the cold, he was so steamed up. And Sandy has one about driving home with a pound of dope in her trunk, stuff she'd grown on a friend's farm and the cops stopping her because one headlight was out and her putting on such a convincing helpless female act, they not only didn't give her a ticket, they took her over to Canadian Tire, helped her install a new headlight and never even thought of checking her trunk.

If I were someone like Rodney Crowell, I could write about how stories are the truckstops on the highway of life. Bright light, black coffee, the other drivers sitting around shooting the shit. Trying to get it straight – what we figure out over the miles, everything that need and distance make of us. There's always a song like that on the radio because someone's always going somewhere or missing someplace or leaving someone and we'll never come to the end of it.

How far we have to go to get even the simplest things. Last summer, it was Susan, showing up at my place after driving all night just to get to me. Just to tell me what she'd found, out there, after 30 years – the little girl whose older brother used to climb into her bed at night, the scar on his chin and how he got it, the blood and cum and crying filling her throat, the fear that had coated her mouth like a fever all her life.

After she left, I drove miles and miles, searching for one house or field that hadn't changed, but everything swam into the heat, thick and watery, like the shakiness that pulled me over to the shoulder, made me sit there with the motor trembling while my cells took what she'd told me in, a little deeper. Sometimes, I'd hear the song crying *(out on the road that lies before me now, there are some turns where I will spin)* and I'd wish it could be that simple *(I only hope that you can hold me now, till I can gain control again)* the distances we have to travel toward each other. So simple you'd almost think it was easy.

Always, I am amazed at what we tell, how much faith we put in it. Never really knowing who is listening, how they're going to take it, where.

COWBOY ANGEL

Out with the truckers and the kickers and the cowboy angels is the line from a Gram Parsons song that always leads me straight to the man I fell in love with one time on a train, in the winter, heading into the mountains out of Edmonton, taking me to Vancouver to look for a job and him as far as Kamloops for his sister's wedding. We met in the bar car. He was wearing silver-toed boots and a black cowboy hat and when I look for him now, that's what I see – a gleam that polishes the glowing dark and a dark hat floating beside me.

We flew straight across that rivered bridge last night, half-past two is how the song puts it. How remembering, like dreaming, is a way of driving all night, billboards and truck-stops flashing past with the voices on the radio, the miles bringing them in and letting them out into the smell of rain, the crying of a train whistle somewhere. Somewhere out there. Where the last arc of a conductor's flash-light rounds us and flows on over the other passengers, their dark, rich breathing filling the curves and hollows of their sleep, until the sun comes up, bringing the mountains with it, the wait in the thick, hot smoke from the brakes, his cigarettes, our kisses, my cowboy angel stepping off into clouds that carry him away as the train starts up again, light rushing out over rocks and the branches of trees, snow flying faster and faster no matter how fast I go.

Out with the truckers and the kickers and the cowboy angels is a line from that Gram Parsons song that Emmylou Harris sings on *Last Date*, the way she always strings a Parsons number onto every album, beads to measure out the years since his death. It's the line that I lean into now, as I leaned then into one last glimpse, there on the platform – that swath of colour that just might be him, heading for the taxi stand on the corner, all the white he's going to leave when he turns it.

FROM NASHVILLE TO MAMMOTH CAVE

All I know of Tennessee is the airport at Nashville, which is just like any airport anywhere, fluorescent light and my life on fast-forward, abrupt and public as the high-gloss glitter on the luggage dropping onto that whirlaround thing, spinning out all the possibilities of chance meetings, Technicolor departures. All that and Elvis too, he was everywhere – that's how you knew it was Tennessee – summing up the state on T-shirts and coffee mugs, life-size in plastic and cardboard, as if you could cram enough of him in after his death to flesh out the rumour he was still alive, so much happening before the flash of my friend's arms, the parking lot, her car and the bright lights of The Grand Ole Opry on my left, heading into Kentucky, where moonlight made the grass even bluer than I could have imagined.

Next morning, it was green again, like the grass back home, the trees in the distance tinged with pink – it was October – like all the trees I've ever seen, at that time of the year. But the light, the light, I like to believe, was Kentucky light, the colour of good corn whiskey, slow and luminous as the accents I was hearing all around me. So when we entered the caves, you can imagine my delight to find that they were pink and green and golden too, although the light was artificial, it was enough for me to see the whole state cut away, like those cross-sections in geography class, or like those lakes back home, when they're that still, trees and pink granite cliffs flying up and down. Without the sky, of course, though I could stretch a bit and say that blue (who knows what or even if), blue was implied by the guide's lesson on how the caves were formed, the oceans whose pull we wouldn't feel were all around us, lives swimming on in the limestone, slow drip of stalactites and the slower reaching up to us of a river somewhere further down through caverns measureless as the time (if we can call it that) it took to make its way here.

Then the guide put the lights out. We were about a quarter of a mile down, maybe thirty-five, forty of us standing there in I want to say "complete darkness" but how, since I want to make you feel it, of course, not see, there was nothing there to, it was – or rather we were – in that darkness closest to silence, *that* silence which has filled out most of this planet's lifetime. Only we, we were not silent, we couldn't be and still *be,* if you see what I mean, or hear, what I did – the gurgle of someone's stomach, my own heart, slow breathing of the man beside me which I took, for the longest time, as my own. Darkness brought us that close. And the cave, of course, the sounds of the body surrounding us, as it used to, the body of the mother everywhere, until the guide, flicking the lights back on, pulled us into ourselves, embarrassed, coughs and laughs pushing our noises back to where we keep them all the rest of our lives.

Outside, the afternoon, straight bourbon, trees suspended in it, making the most of that movement we learn to describe as chemical, chlorophyll giving way to carotin, those oranges which are always there and we can't see for all that green, another way that light deceives us. And in the parking lot, no kidding, there's a busload just in from Nashville, the driver waiting 'till the song is over – *just come on home to your blue Kentucky girl* – before he snaps off the radio, climbs down and leads everyone forward together for the 3 o'clock tour.

BELLYFULL OF BLUEBIRD WINE

You know how music grows from the weather in a place, the lay of the land. Drinking songs especially. Think of that misty rowdiness the Irish settle into or the brisk *oompah* of Oktoberfest and you'll hear what I mean.

In the ones that Emmylou Harris does the tables are covered with arborite – or those little terrycloth covers – soaking wet, smeared with cigarette ashes, chip crumbs, squishy bits of pickled egg. The band is playing "The Last Cheater's Waltz," someone's done you wrong, the bottle's let you down and there's nothing but Sunday between you and the rest of the week. So you knock back another one, hoping it will work, steady drinking like a steady job, if you could just stick at it, it might get you where you want to go.

On the album *Grievous Angel* there are a few cuts of Harris and Parsons singing live in a pub in Northern Quebec. Just as they move into "Hickory Wind" you can hear glass breaking, which is accidental, of course, but not unusual, you can hear it anywhere around here. Glass and hearts and backs and marriages shattering all over the wild side of life, which is the territory these songs cover, like the thick, yellow smoke filling your chest and throat and eyes with an excuse for tears. And another drink, of course.

Which is all right, 'cause it's midnight, and there's two more bottles of wine.

THIS IS THE CLOSEST I COME TO A SONG

Which you can pretty well guess is going to be for all the things I *can't* do, like carry a tune or even my own body very far, my knees, like my voice, arthritic, coded for failure by some ancestor I never met, stiffening into a past I didn't get to choose, though this song being what it is, I'll have to sing for *that,* too, the genetic fluke that sticks me with some tonedeaf, awkward family and everything I have to bear because of it. Which, of course, is your situation too, so that'll bring you in with a few bars about how stupid you used to feel in English class when you couldn't get some poem they were doing, which starts the guy next door off on his sciatica and how he can't grow roses worth a damn and before you know it, we're so hot, we've got Patsy Cline singing the solos, Hank Williams on rhythm, Maybelle Carter on lead, Bill Black on bass, Harris and Parsons, pulling it all together, lots of fiddles and ban-joes, harmonicas, a couple of mandolins, pretty soon there'll be an album, some concerts, a world tour – or do you think I'm taking this too far, that it's all too crazy? Well, what do you think we're doing anyway, spinning out here, stuck with each other and no more able to get over that than we can get over our need for oxygen? Why not sing for what we can't do, instead of all this booming and bragging, most of us stuck in the back row anyway, squawking, gimped-up. What if some tuneless wonder's all we've got to say for ourselves? Off-key, our failings held out, at last, to each other. What else have we got to offer, really? What else do we think they're for?

THE PRESENCE OF JESUS

What I want to call *pentimento,* borrowing that word from another world to show how he shows up here, amid diesel engines, bar stools, clapboard churches, greasy spoons. Resurrected, like the songs themselves, in the dust that rises from the hot fields and endless highways, sticking to the back of your throat, thirsty for the water you can always just see, just up ahead where the horizon shifts and shimmers at the end of another day, the only true companion you can count on. Though to see him like this you have to blot out that ornate agony on a gold cross or the fair-haired hippie in the Sunday School hall, bring up denim and a three-day beard, bronze eyes, gold-flecked, like the tobacco he always hands around, the scent of it – and sweat – haloing him like holiness, a cross between a Wobbly and a saint (remember John Carradine in *The Grapes of Wrath?)* the way the songs themselves make Heaven sound like the One Big Union in the sky.

When Emmylou Harris sings "Jordan" or "When He Comes" or "Where Could I Go but to the Lord" you can hear how easily it happens. The way her voice just reaches out to that spot where the road starts to waver and there, in the sudden, hazy light that dusk brings on, Jesus appears. Out of nowhere, of course, but matter-of-fact about it, rolling a cigarette or stopping to blow his nose, like he's been doing this for ages and figures that sooner or later someone will catch on. The other thing is that the song isn't at all surprised to know this about him, only you are and it's just as you figure *this* out, of course, that he looks straight at you, fades to the old familiar dirt and sky, the song fading too, that voice growing into the world in the casual way that trees or angels manage, leaving you still here, still getting the hang of it.

WHERE THE SWEETHEART RIDES THE RODEO AGAIN

Rock of ages cleft for me
I swung down my hammer out in Joshua Tree
It rang on the mountain and rolled to the sea
And it will ring when they bury me.

– *Emmylou Harris, "Sweet Chariot,"*
The Ballad of Sally Rose

Thinking of Gram Parsons, his death in 1973 in Joshua Tree, California, OD'd on those "personal demons that haunted his whole life" as one bio puts it, and how "still unknown individuals stole his coffin … and burned it near Joshua Tree Monument."

Burning his body, the greasy smoke from it sticking to the wind, clogging their throats with whatever was left in him of the raw mix of carelessness and longing that burns through his songs and in the same breath chokes him. Smoke settling in the air that anyone can breathe, as his songs fill the lungs of anyone who takes them in, rising in Emmylou Harris's voice to the top of the charts, flowing on into her own music, "Boulder to Birmingham," or *The Ballad of Sally Rose* blooming from his dying as each of us blooms from the deaths that nourish us and let us go, the deaths we survive.

Hearing her sing like that, my chest tightens, thick with all those voices I cannot name and never acknowledge. How I take whole lives in in an afternoon, sitting around listening, drinking coffee, watching the light drift from the pine trees to the garden, touching each thing it rests on freely, as we, sometimes, are able to touch.

How it was wanting brought me to these poems. Wanting them to embrace that voice as I embrace my lover's body, to be shaped by everything they meet, the way I am shaped by my son, even now, as he grows taller than me into his own life. The obvious, unavoidable weight of it, how we fill each other briefly, but perfectly and then uncurl, from arms, wombs, lungs, as carelessly as smoke uncurls across the sky. Even the dead, whose dying goes on and on.

Everyday Science

RHYTHM AND GENES

We all hear – though we may not be conscious of – the beat that thrums through every human conversation. *Rhythmic synchrony* it's called, our sync sense, which, like the other five, conducts us through the worlds we make of each other, or in this case, sets us dancing in each other's stops and starts, digressions, turns and leaps of thought, hyperbole, lies, warnings, lovers' cries – we move to music, and the scientists who study this sort of thing (sociolinguistic microanalysts they call themselves) can clock the tempo with a metronome, and score it, too, each eighth note, triplet, rest and syncopation measured as a waltz or a square-dance. The word's melody and the body's, too: the eyebrows going up or down, the chin's jut, fingers' flex, hands in the air and shoulders coming in on the shrug – it's all there and what's more, they say, it's vital to what we listen to, or how. Why, some of them would even claim we learned it way back when, a bunch of us hunting mastodons, say, and needing to know how to throw our spears in unison, on the beat, or hear the cry, clearing its way through all the other cries, that warned us our young were in danger. Such music's all around us, seeded by our mothers' heartbeats, dreamy and persistent as those water-memories we know we have, of being born. It keeps us constantly in auditory touch: in less than 14 milliseconds thoughts in my head translate to muscular movements in my throat and mouth, to airways by which your eardrum oscillates in absolute synchrony with my voice. So you can see how easily the whole thing flies apart if we listen only to the meaning of the words. Most microanalysts would say that we could end lovers' quarrels, racial conflicts, even the possibility of nuclear war, right now, today, if we'd just go with the music, which is everywhere and everything, the pulse of the atom, the singing of the spheres.

All of which brings us to Dr Susumu Ohno, a geneticist in California who has assigned each base of DNA – that's adenine, guanine, cytosine and thymine – musical notes, from which he composes pieces like "Calcium Pump of Rabbit Muscle" or "Mouse RNA

Polymerase II," catchy little tunes that grow more complicated with evolution, so that one-cell protozoa translate to simple four-note repetitions, while a complex slime may be a two-step. And – wait, there's more – it works the other way, too, a Chopin piece transcribes into the formula for a human cancer gene. And all of this flows, of course, into what microanalysts say about how the beat doesn't come from the music anyway, but from us, a hit song releasing in everyone a sort of rhythmic consensus. So that you could say that the music we use to heal ourselves or bury ourselves, send someone off to war or marriage is actually composed of tears or adrenalin or those gushy swooshes of the heart that push us into each other's arms. Or heads, lungs, eyes, this poem moving into that rhythm which releases you to go and change the baby or the record, catch a bus, take out the garbage. When I think, you could say it's a scientific fact: how, for a moment in there, maybe two or three milliseconds, your body moves to the beat my thought set up, just as my hand writes by what it hears of you, out there somewhere. You should almost say that, for a millisecond anyway, we both consent to this, with our whole selves, every strand alight and quivering.

BODILY FLUIDS

I'm working on this theory that the way we think is directly related to the brain's being 80% water. It's an ocean up there, thoughts drifting, shifting on the currents of scent and sound, past lives surfacing like drowned bodies when you least expect, poems nuzzling idle in pools to see what light makes of those hours in the middle of an afternoon, the whole mind, coming up, just once, in a splash of sun and air, eyes, lungs, a single organ in the glare of a Big Idea.

And then there are those schools of slithery thought where most of us spend most of our time, just swimming along. Like the other day, I'm giving blood at the Legion Hall, for the Red Cross, and I drift into that woozy part of it – you know, after they've taken the needle out, but before they let you up for the doughnuts and coffee, when you're lying there holding the gauze to your arm, like at the dentist, after he's packed your mouth, whipped off your bib and said *okay see you in two weeks* and you're still trying to concentrate on standing up. Well, I'm floating there, surrounded by all these bags of blood and naturally I start meandering along the routes it will take from here, mine flowing into some guy who cuts his finger off in his Cuisinart, say, some banker who thinks nurses are over-paid and everyone on welfare is a lazy slob, while the guy beside me here could be pumping his pint straight into the arms of a radical feminist who figures if they can put one man on the moon, why not all of them, it was almost like drowning, how the possibilities came rushing through me. Even the nurse said to lie down for a while more and someone else brought me a Coke. One sip and I dive into how much of it is drunk by Canadians in a single day, enough to fill two Olympic swimming pools and how the friend who told me that – who knows where she gets this stuff – also claims that the semen ejaculated in one year, in heterosexual intercourse alone, would fill another one-and-a-half and that's just in England and Wales, while the water that evaporates from the earth's oceans in one day fills five. I could feel it, surging around my heart, the nurse's smile wobbly, like the sun in a puddle, no telling where it would flash next, as she launches me toward the doughnuts.

I eddy up alongside this table, sit down, and the guy across from me looks up from his paper and says, "You know what kills more people than cigarettes?" "No." "Loneliness." And he shows me the article, his fingers, indignant, darting through the words as if they'd seeped right out of his own head, taking me off around islands, whales beaching themselves, the sharp, grey warnings dolphins offer. I had so little to give him, so little time, before he heaved himself up and shoved off, leaving cigarette butts, doughnut crumbs, his blood in a bag in a fridge back there, his newspaper, open – *Surgeons Discover Sea Coral Best Substitute for Human Face Bones* – me, looking up from this, just as he pushes the door out into the afternoon, the heat, the light washing over him.

NEWS OF THE DEAD

I've stopped reading the daily newspapers, switched to those tabloids you get at the check-out counter. Out of respect for the dead. I mean, in the dailies, they don't even get a verb. "Peacefully, after a long illness." "Suddenly, as the result of an accident." No alternative but to freeze into attitudes, kids playing statues. Or as if the voice of doom just calls your number and, *poof*, you're out of here, no trouble at all, this coming to the very end.

That could never happen in the tabloids. In the tabs, being dead is the same as being alive, only the other way around, like a negative, where people's faces are hard to make out, but have this light around them, like the faces of angels. So it makes sense to have a regular feature called "Star Talk from Beyond the Grave," giving answers to your problems from people who are really there. Sharon Tate on forgiveness (no). Mae West on sex (yes). A kind of think-tank full of experts, only these experts have dying on their résumé. It gives their expertise that extra *whoosh,* like really hot breath on the frosted window of opportunity. You can see the possibilities. Imagine Anne Boleyn on upward mobility, John Keats on miracle drugs, after all these years.

And another thing. The dead have had it with being totted up and deducted, in a few columns, while the undead go on, smiling the same smiles, under the same headlines, in every daily in the world. The tabloids nurture the dead. Just look at Billy Curmano. From a coffin, lowered with elaborate ceremony into the ground of Rushford, Minnesota, he lies in "the haunted darkness" singing, reciting poetry and dancing horizontally for them, while in Kalamazoo, Michigan, the ghost of a dead grandmother lives on in an egg which the family stores carefully in the fridge. And in Chapel Hill, North Carolina, Lewis St Louis says that "the dead are one of our most abundant natural resources." He uses them to make beautiful things, his most notable being a "Postmortem Portrait of Andy Warhol," which features a human skull (not Andy's) studded with Coca-Cola caps and semi-precious stones.

The dailies can't manage that, though they use the dead, just the same. And then go on acting as if the dead were dead, while the tabs offer scientific proof that there's more to it than that. 1/3000th of an ounce, to be exact. Which is the difference in weight between a live body and a dead one, after you've allowed for air leaving the lungs and instantaneous physical deterioration. It is the precise weight of the soul, a fact you'd never find in the dailies.

It is unlikely the dailies are going to change on any of this, though it will eventually be bad for business. Meanwhile the tabs will continue providing the only significant news of the dead and I will continue reading it. The dead themselves will continue granting interviews and giving advice. They will show up in the oddest places. The residue from their bodies will continue shining from our windows at night and firing the rockets that send us off into outer space. Where some people believe the dead live, though the evidence only reaches us long after they've taken off for somewhere else, someplace they've just heard about, from a distance, after all these years.

MIRACLES

If Jesus were coming to this town, he would have come
somewhere different than on a damn freezer.
– John Gaul, Mayor
Estill Springs, Tenn.

I don't think of her as a tulku. *I just think of her as my mom.*
– Ben Burroughs, son of Catharine
Burroughs, Ahkon Lhamo

Sometimes I don't know whether to be grateful or terrified.
– Patricia Sieler, owner of a velvet painting
of Elvis that weeps real tears

And that's what most of us
balk at, I suppose. Not knowing
whether to be grateful or terrified
we reject the case of Arlene Gardner's GE
on which the face of Christ appears
effortlessly. As the face of Mildred
appears whenever I hear the word
mundane, her hand, writing *mundus, munda*
on the blackboard, the chalk-dust
Clearasil smell of the classroom,
me tuning in, the tongues of the dead
singing on, *M.K. loves T.J. True.*
Forever. rough-cut, on my desk.
But – to return to Jesus, there
on the freezer – you can see
the problems he causes, especially given
Mrs Gardner's testimony ("God revealed
to me that he made the freezer
into a TV") which reveals so little
of divine intent. We can't blame the neighbours
for complaining about people on crutches
cluttering their front lawns.

So the Gardners plan to move the freezer,
just as Patricia Sieler plans
to give the painting (which cries
when she plays "Heartbreak Hotel," cheers up
on "Jailhouse Rock") to a museum.
"I can't keep something like this
to myself," she says. Which,
of course, she can't. Any more than
Catharine Burroughs, mother of three,
can be kept from the recognition
that she is the re-incarnation of a
Buddhist saint. "The Brooklyn girl in me
was surprised by what happened," she tells us.
"But the rest of me wasn't." And I can see it,
how we all try to make sense of ourselves
that way, which parts we hold on to, which
we hold at arms' length, squinting,
just as we do the photo
of that face some people see
on Mars these days, seeing if we can
make it into mountains. What else
can we do? It's centuries since the word
mirari, to wonder at, began to blur
through the French *mirer*, into *mirare*,
to regard intently. As I used to – if you'll
remember Miss Caughey – the blackboard, *mundus*
clouded by the next day's homework,
Thursday's Glee Club practice, disappearing
effortlessly, as the light drew
our afternoon away, all of us
poised for the bell.
But. Having said all that,
I still can't keep to myself
what happened to me once: on the anniversary,
to the day, of a friend's death, she appeared,
in the laundromat where I was folding underwear,
by the dryer, putting in a load of towels.

I didn't know what to do. I kept
staring and she kept being there.
Until she turned, of course, and
turned into someone else, one of those faulty
appearances you've caught in your own
face, probably, in anyone's, shadowy
comfort I tried to make
for myself that day, nothing
to wonder at. It's just how we look
at the world sometimes, tensed
with the effort that makes our brains
hurt, all that work, rejecting what
the senses tell us. No wonder we think
we have to look so hard. No wonder
we stand here, blinking.
Grateful and terrified. Like the one
man police force in Estill Springs,
Tennessee. All that traffic, backed up
clear to the highway, for a glimpse
of the GE Jesus.

Early Poems

FOR A SISTER

Finally the dishes are done,
                    Floor swept
Children bathed and put to bed.
At last there is time for coffee, cigarettes
                And quiet talk between us.
("Woman stuff" – the men would say).
Tonight you tell me how it was when you
            were young and single (as the saying goes)
Describing parties, dances, love affairs
Your face alive and laughing
With memories of what seems far away –
Until you rise, your body heavy with another child,
And I remember:
                    You are not yet twenty.

LABOUR HEARING

(Poem for Mike L)

"I remember it was hot that day
– ninety-five degrees at least –
No guard on the machine – a guy could lose his arm –
And then, a man laid off left two to do the work of three –
It can't be done! the line's too fast –
So when I saw the others walking out –
        I wanted to be with them –
        I left my work and went …"

Words like thick brushes –
        adequate for outlines only –
A few flat strokes that stubbornly exclude
        so many inarticulate dimensions
That the recreated scene hangs awkwardly upon the air –
        a lifeless shadow of itself.
The court is silent as the prosecuting lawyer leans complacently
        towards his victim:
  "Surely, witness, there is more than that.
  You saw a group of men and followed them;
  What then? What further explanation …"
Secure within his knowledge of the law,
        he twists and jabs –
    badgers the man for details –
Sifts through his words for something more precise,
        some legal phrase to circumscribe
  confusing situations, partially glimpsed
That somehow – vaguely – threaten him,
And yet remain incomprehensible.
He concentrates on words.
The thing he seeks flows past the words –
        past anger, past frustration –

To forces palpable and solid as the man before him –
          a man who owns what he will never find,
Who smiles as he remembers –
A factory withering to silence
          amid the shouts and laughter of a crowd of men.

THE BABY SHOWER

Mid-afternoon on a Sunday
cups and spoons laid out on the best cloth
coffee perking on the stove
presents piled pink and blue and yellow on a nearby table
The guest of honour bulges in a straight-backed chair
while round her that relentless sisterhood
begin their rites:

"This is the worst time now, dear. The waiting.
I know just how you feel. I was terrified myself.
But it's all over soon enough – if you're lucky."

"Yeh – if you're lucky. Christ, I was
        eighteen hours with Kevin and they
        wouldn't even let me have a glass of water."

"I went twenty-four before they did a section. Swore
I'd never have another. But Tom wanted a boy so
badly, I …"

"It's easy for the men to talk; they don't
        have to go through it. Not me, boy. Never
        again."

"And that's only the beginning. God, if I had to raise
my two again – ten months apart, I must have been nuts –
I'd kill myself …"

        "Or keep your legs crossed …"

"Yeh …"

Grimly, they continue their litany

of unspeakable horrors
mothers, sisters, next-door neighbours
are routinely mutilated
their shrieks of agony grow palpable
above the clink of coffee cups   fall
to a silence
as another chant begins   subtle
      strong   and equally relentless:

"Oh, but they're
the best years of your life!"

            "The most quickly forgotten pain in the world."

"The day my youngest started school
I cried all morning"

            "Nothing like that first smile!"

"The first steps …"

            "I've still got a lock of Brian's hair
and I'm a grandmother now."

"The best years of my life, dear.
Don't let anyone tell you different."

Cake is served now   gifts are opened
tiny caps and sweaters
diapers   nightgowns   pass
hand to hand around the circle
Someone says "Remember the seventh gift opened
is the next mother!"
and in the corner someone else blushes and laughs
Eyes meet   knowing smiles   and again
someone   "It's about time!"

About time you joined us
we are waiting
to initiate you   we
will be cruel   advise you
frighten you   until
you hate us   it is necessary
that we do   there is
no other way for us to understand
what has been done to us   how
from our first birth   we are
changed   are never
the same again   that knowing
we would share with you
but ours is not the language
of baby books   we did not
write them   make instead
this ritual   that we might
repeat ourselves   hold to it
that we might   survive.

They leave now   gather coats and handbags
hurry off to relieve babysitters and husbands
make supper   bathe the children
From her chair the guest of honour
thanks each for her gift   as she waves goodbye
her eyes grow distant   the hand on the belly listens
for that first tightening   inside
the baby   stubbornly and silently
kicks back

SENTIMENTAL POEM FOR MY MOTHER

I grew up on
how your father lost the farm
during the Depression so that you
couldn't go to university   but I
must   which I did   became
a statistic of the sixties
marched to ban bombs   end wars
discovered Marx and Women's Liberation
abortion   marijuana   brown rice
moved as far as I could
from the suburbs   out from that
yellow split-level house
you bought when I was fifteen
to downtown apartments
where macramé hangings
cover cracks in the plaster
and dirty window panes
are filled with plants
moved out but never away
from our first night there
you amid packing cases
running your hand through
beige shag carpeting
crying "I love this house, I love
this house"
after years in cramped apartments
a guest in your own dream

Your tears embarrassed me
and I am still
embarrassed by the memory   still
I carry it   look cautiously
at my own child   waiting
what shape it will take
in us

YOU'VE COME A LONG WAY, BABY!

Ten years ago   on the quiet campus
of a small-town university
I was
one of Them
braless and bluejeaned
hair flying around my face   I
stormed into senate meetings
shook my fist in the faces
of mild-eyed academics   and demanded
that students have
  – representation on faculty committees
  – decision power over course content
  – relevant courses
  – the power to evaluate professors (with the guarantee
that the results carry weight in decisions of
tenure, firing, etc.)

Ten years later   on another quiet campus
in another town   I sit
bra-ed and mascaraed
hair in a smooth coil round my head
my smile appropriate
for the secretary
of a liberal department   where the professors
are often bearded   and sometimes
wear blue jeans
Today I type the forms
 (in triplicate)
for the student evaluations
of departmental courses.
These will be placed in sealed envelopes
 (which I also have to type)
distributed to classes by student representatives

(chosen by acclamation when
there was insufficient interest
for an election)
who hate distributing the forms
as much as I hate typing them.
The forms will then go
to the computer centre   where other secretaries
will code them
and return the results
in sealed envelopes
a kind of Academic Awards Night
which is not televised
and where everyone gets an Oscar.

I take a coffee break
over a second cigarette   meditate
the smaller ironies of life
and later that afternoon   realize
I'll have to work overtime but
since I'm not unionized
I won't even get
time and a half.

DEPARTURES

It's these conversations
we keep having
trying to have
about love   about how
to love each other

In the back of our minds love
is that place you get to
and remain in somehow
like the prince and the princess
smiling into the blank page
at the end of the fairy tale
the blank page where they will live
happily ever after

a place like that still
in the back of our minds
despite the break-ups among our friends
the accidents that happen
to other people   love still
that rosy haven and the language
just a map we use to get there
like the ones we memorized in school
familiar as our home towns

We never expect what happens
although it always does   the first word
between us that alters
everything   even the light
shatters   the air suddenly
stark and dangerous

In the back of my mind somewhere
I want you to be the shining
knight   the youngest son who always wins

the girl but you open your mouth
become the eldest brother
who beats the wise old woman
tricks the dwarf the one
who never catches on
I try to tell you this and watch
as you crash around inside
my female grammar like someone lost
in an impossible myth he has to get through
win some boon from whoever he imagines
living there

I love you
we keep saying
I love you
as if the words were magic
carpets could transport us
to wherever it is
we think we want to go

In the back of our minds
love was a place you could count on
a promise the language made
but in these conversations
we keep trying to have
each word becomes an opening
a treacherous possibility
what we might be
might not

LIKE THE PETIT POINT

Like the petit point our grandmothers
worked at in the evenings   the lace
trimmed nightgown saved for the odd
hours when the other work was done
eyes strained against the dim light
of a lamp the tiny stitches
while the men talked politics and crops
or dozed beside the fire

our friendship even now in
the last third of the twentieth century
after the suffrage movement the meetings
and rallies the books we've read
still like that
something we put aside for our
children our lovers or husbands
our other work   something we pick up
when we can
                    and even then
sometimes it looks as frivolous
as our grandmother's lace not
practical like bread or canned tomatoes
not even necessary
you might say when we go out
for a drink and men we scarcely know
intrude   standing there
expectant their drinks in one hand
the other poised to move their chairs
to our table and that look in their eyes
that even now assumes
the friendship of women
is something to put by
when something more important
comes along
                    intruding

even when they aren't there
evenings at your place or mine
the children finally put to bed
the supper dishes stacked
on the drainboard and quiet
around us a gift sweet
tea in our cups even then
we talk about them and they tangle
through our conversation like the sturdy wool
of that good warm sweater we never quite
finish though we think we should

it's not as easy as we thought
putting that work by even
with the books the poems we read
to each other about strong women

and yet in those odd hours
of our friendship we grow
frivolous as schoolgirls sometimes
laughter gleams like bright threads
between us and often
we couldn't even say what
we're giggling about it's more
what we discover here
like the herb garden you found
when you moved to that old house
and spent a whole day weeding it
when you could have been planting
sensible beans and tomatoes
thinking of your grandmother's petit point
and how the herbs would hang in your kitchen
spreading their pungent laughter
through all your winter rooms

WE ALL HAVE DREAMS

We all have dreams
we can't remember   dreams
which take us down so deep
that words we think we've never spoken
fill our mouths   the dark rooms
echo with them and we wake
thinking someone has called us
one of the children perhaps
but our children are all asleep
hands cupped beneath their smooth dry cheeks

there are no places we go at night
and return from   finding
the pillow damp with what might be tears
"Did I cry in my sleep
last night?" we ask
but the faces of our husbands our wives
remain smooth as the milk jug on the breakfast table
they can only talk of how we mutter
when we lie on our backs
their practical wisdom sliding
away from us while stranger phrases
tangle through our thoughts
like half-forgotten songs

There are countries we travel through
in darkness and emerge from changed
not in a way our mirrors can register
though what we see there makes us glad
for the morning news   the crisp
well-chosen words that map
a planet's natural disasters
give us weather we can understand
so that we venture out
muffled against a known cold

we all have dreams
we think we can't remember
and glad for the first thin light
that hardens into day
we enter each morning careless
as children who test the first good ice of winter
on a pond somewhere
with nothing but a kind of stubborn trust
to hold them from the dark mouths
deeper than their mothers' warnings
opening beneath their feet

THESE THINGS HAPPEN

and the TV news records
the discovery of a new born
baby whose mother left him
in a Salvation Army used
clothing bin in downtown Detroit

but not how her face
looked   empty curve of her
hands as the lid banged shut
sharp metal echo through the
dark streets the city closing
in around her

the reports are indignant
although they wouldn't be if
she'd seen him off to war and he'd
been killed   then
we'd see her face
that lost bewildered look
such women have as they
lay flowers on some
monument

these things happen
and the official language
indicates their meanings
although in other words
it comes to the same thing
flesh has its own vocabulary
the dulled eyes and broken
gestures of a woman's hands
that speak of how the life
she makes
can be sloughed off

like an old suit
something that doesn't fit
and nothing ever new
or ever really
her own

THEY SAY THERE'S ALWAYS A WORST

They say there's always a worst and then you're through.
"You're over the worst of it," they told me,
ten days after the accident
that left me a body they thought they could fix,
a piece of equipment with a few faulty parts
they'd teach me the names for, all over again.
"This is your arm," they said, "this is how it works."
And they were right, it did, but it wasn't the same.
This tension in my shoulder muscles,
stiff with the work of holding the arm in place
is what doctors call *protective reflex*.
A fancy phrase which means
that the body forgets nothing,
like saying *I can feel it in my bones*
when we speak of a warning we don't quite understand.

They say there's always a worst
and you work it through.
"I'm done with that," my friend says
of her divorce, "I've worked it out."
A mathematical problem in the end,
pain you can quantify and go on
to the next page.
Even dying has its stages,
people discuss them at cocktail parties.
Death is what you come to terms with.
You *come to terms,* as if you could accept
the conditions, what they mean.

Like a man I knew who said he'd held death in his arms.
I couldn't believe him,
though I understood his need:
words he could get his mouth around,
a phrase for the safety of it.
You can hold on to *death,* after all,

but sooner or later you have to say
my mother or *my wife* or even *my child;*
sooner or later you have to give it
a name you love.

They say the worst is what you get over,
but there's always the private reckoning
when the days come ragged,
like the breath of a woman I loved
when she was dying, a breathing
that made its own silence at last,
giving death her face
which I will never see again.

I'm told you get over this, like anything else,
and after a while, you accept.
"Things change," they tell me, "life goes on."
But even the body's cells, renewing every seven years,
repeat the same old story. All of it.
The bones tend their history of pain
and no one knows when it will come
or how often: rising in the season of its need
this grief that breaks, fiercely
and without warning.

LIKE ALL OF OUR FRIENDS

All of our friends are breaking up
or wanting to. It's ugly to watch
the women's eyes darken in their sockets
and the men's faces stain
with that awkward weariness
that only men seem to endure.
It's all the damage.
Not just the desperate kind
that words can do – holes torn
in promises and the crude thrusts
that violate memories – but furniture thrown
in broken heaps on a front lawn, a knot of bruises
on a woman's breast and glass crushed
into a man's palm.

For days now, words
have tumbled in my head
like the sound of the ocean
in an old poem: "Ah, love, let us be true
To one another!"

If I close my eyes, I can almost
see them, lovers standing by a window,
gleam of light on the French coast, gleam
of their love against the dark,
the ignorant armies clashing by night.

Ah, love, let us be true.

Before all this damage started
we learned that poem in high school,
most of us. The distant voices
of English teachers and the remote
innocence of another century. All that wisdom
we can't use.

I watch your hands move
around the smooth outlines of things,
arranging books, peeling an orange.
I am in love with your hands. They know
the coiled secrets of my body and your tongue
speaks my thoughts almost before
I think them. We understand
what happens in each other's eyes.

I watch your hands, remembering
the other things I know about them,
the holes they have punched
in other women's walls, the ragged edges
your words have left. You know the same
about mine.

There are promises we can't make
to each other. It isn't a matter
of will or honour. It's more organic
than that, a fault in the blood,
a lost gene.

Whatever.

There are distances between men and women
that promises can't fill anymore.

Ah, love, man of the beautiful
hands. We understand so well
what happens in each other's eyes
that we can see it there
already: the ignorant
dark that waits
to blind us to each other someday.
Violently.
Like too much light.

Annotations

p. 38 Judah River, Amy Snow: the two eldest children of Pat Logan.

p. 61 Liz Whynot, Linde Zingaro: older sister of Chris Whynot (Bronwen's life partner), and her life partner.

p. 88 Carole: Carole Patry, friend of Bronwen's, long-term nurse in OB/GYN unit at Kingston General Hospital.

p. 97 No. 7: highway crossing Ontario from Sarnia to Ottawa. Ompah and Plevna are rural villages in the township of North Frontenac.

p. 137 UEL: United Empire Loyalists, American settlers loyal to the British Empire, many of whom settled in what is now Canada following the American Revolution.

p. 145 Harrowsmith: a small rural community north of Kingston, in South Frontenac township.

Tamworth: a rural community thirty-nine kilometres northwest of Harrowsmith.

The drive north on Highway 38 passes through Harrowsmith, then Hartington, turns west at Verona on Highway 14, passing Bellrock, Enterprise, turning north at County Road 4, and finally reaching Tamworth within the Township of Stone Mills. The Wallace family farm and the former one-room schoolhouse at which Marguerite (Wagar) Wallace worked are located on the west side of Highway 38, just north of Harrowsmith.

p. 149 Uncle Cam: Cameron Wallace, Bronwen's brother and only sibling, born in Kingston in December 1949.

p. 154 "a volcano erupts": El Chichón, in Chiapas, Mexico, erupted in spring 1982, causing the largest volcanic disaster in the country's modern history.

p. 163 Virginia Beach: a coastal city in southeastern Virginia situated where the Chesapeake Bay meets the Atlantic Ocean.
p. 185 Mary di Michele: a friend and fellow writer, author of novels and poetry, including *Bread and Chocolate,* published in a joint collection with Bronwen's *Marrying into the Family* (Oberon Press, 1980).
p. 193 Mark: Mark Buchner, Windsor resident and friend.
RenCen: The Renaissance Center, Detroit, Michigan. Construction on these seven interconnected skyscrapers began in 1973 on the International Riverfront. The Renaissance Center complex is owned by General Motors and operates as its world headquarters.
p. 194 Wyandotte: a road in Windsor, running east–west, just south of the Detroit River.
p. 196 Jan Conn: a friend, poet, and entomologist.
p. 198 Chris: Chris Whynot, Bronwen's life partner.
p. 199 Pat: Pat Logan, friend, mother of Amy, Judah, Jason, and Leah.
p. 200 Carolyn: Carolyn Smart, friend, poet.
p. 205 Jeremy: Jeremy Baxter, Bronwen and Ron Baxter's son, born in Windsor in 1974.
Elven Cloak, Gauntlets of Ogre Power, Great Tree, Wind Wailer, Bag of Devouring: magical elements in Dungeons & Dragons, a fantasy tabletop role-playing game developed in 1974.
Anat: a fierce Semitic war goddess, from multiple mythological sources.
p. 215 Jim Rhodes: friend.
Peter Mathewson: fictional name.
p. 217 John and Lindy Stevenson: friends. John was a colleague when Bronwen taught at St Lawence College, Kingston.
Roger: fictional name.
p. 218 Doug: fictional name.
p. 220 Lorraine: fictional name.
p. 229 Isabel Huggan, friend, author of fiction and personal essays.
p. 240 Peter D: Peter Dyson-Bonter, 1948–1984, married to Bronwen between 1967 and 1969.

p. 243 Julie Cruikshank: a Canadian anthropologist who collaborates with Indigenous peoples of Yukon in her research on oral traditions.

Carcross, NWT: Carcross, formerly Caribou Crossing, is a community in Yukon between Bennett Lake and Nares Lake.

Caribou Hotel: a Yukon historic site in Carcross.

p. 246 Marty and Jessie Glaberman: Martin Glaberman was a legendary figure in Detroit radical circles and both he and Jessie Glaberman were important mentors for Bronwen in the 1970s.

p. 255 Hotel Dieu: one of two major hospitals in the Kingston area.

Interval House: an emergency shelter and second-stage housing facility for women, children, and youth experiencing violence.

p. 257 ECU: extreme close-up, a cinematographer's term.

p. 262 Argentina: on 24 March 1976, a military junta led by General Jorge Rafael Videla seized power from President Isabel Perón. Between 1976 and 1983 it is estimated that 30,000 people whom the new government suspected of involvement with left-wing activities were "disappeared" by authorities in what is now called the "Dirty War."

p. 263 Lorna Crozier: friend and poet.

Clifford Olson: convicted serial killer of children and young adults, incarcerated for many years in Kingston.

Kingston Pen: Kingston Penitentiary, a maximum-security prison for men in Kingston.

P4W: Prison for Women, a maximum-security prison for women in Kingston.

p. 271 Holly Near: an American singer-songwriter and activist.

p. 274 Barb: Barb Carey, friend, poet, journalist.

p. 278 Koko, Ameslan: Koko was a gorilla who was taught to converse in American Sign Language, or Ameslan.

Mr Ed: a talking horse, the title character of a television series, 1961–66.

Reagan and Gorbachev in Geneva: The Geneva Summit took place 19 and 20 November 1985 when US president Ronald

Reagan met with Soviet general secretary Mikhail Gorbachev for the first time to discuss international diplomatic relations and the arms race.

p. 279 Jane Goodall: primatologist and anthropologist, considered to be the world's foremost expert on chimpanzees.

p. 281 Kathie: Kathie Wallace, Bronwen's cousin, who grew up on the family farm in Harrowsmith.

Ferron: Canadian singer-songwriter and poet. Bronwen requested that Ferron's music be played at her memorial service. Her song "Proud Crowd Pride Cried" ended the memorial; Emmylou Harris's song "From Boulder to Birmingham" began it.

p. 287 Ron: Ron Baxter, Bronwen's partner; labour activist; father of Jeremy Baxter, Bronwen's only child.

p. 288 Mike Longmoore: friend; labour activist in Windsor; Ford worker.

p. 292 Philippe Petit: French high-wire artist who in 1974 walked across a wire between the Twin Towers of the World Trade Center.

Houdini's dying promise: Harry Houdini, the illusionist, promised his wife that he would return from the dead with a coded message.

Annie Edson Taylor: the first person to survive a trip over the Horseshoe Falls at Niagara in a barrel.

La Quebrada: a major tourist attraction in Acapulco, Mexico, where divers entertain tourists by jumping from perilous cliffs, forty and eighty feet high.

Zacchini: Hugo Zacchini, a human cannonball, the first to use a compressed-air cannon.

p. 295 Gibbard sideboard: the Gibbard Furniture Company, founded by John Gibbard in Napanee, Ontario, in 1835, was the oldest furniture maker in Canada when it closed in 2010.

p. 298 Charlie Saunders: fictitious name.

p. 300 John Fogerty: American singer-songwriter, founder of the band Creedence Clearwater Revival.

p. 307 Winfield Scott: American songwriter.

p. 311 Gram Parsons, Rodney Crowell, Kitty Wells, Chuck Berry, Merle Haggard, Dolly Parton, Patsy Cline, Jesse Winchester: American singer-songwriters.

p. 312 Jim, Sandy, Susan: fictitious names.

p. 315 The Grand Ole Opry: a weekly country music stage concert in Nashville, Tennessee, founded in 1925. It is the longest-running radio broadcast in US history. The current venue, the Opryland House, is located at 2804 Opryland Drive in Nashville.

p. 317 Bluebird Wine: the bluebird.com website states: "Bluebird Wines exists to produce amazing California wines that real people can enjoy every day."

p. 318 Hank Williams, Maybelle Carter, Bill Black: American singer-songwriters and musicians.

p. 319 Wobbly: member of the Industrial Workers of the World, an international labour union founded in 1905 in Chicago.

John Carradine: American actor who played the role of a former preacher, Jim Casy, in the film of the John Steinbeck novel *The Grapes of Wrath.* Casy becomes a labour organizer and tries to recruit for a union with tragic results.

One Big Union: a Canadian trade union active primarily in the west, formed in Calgary on 4 June 1919, and merging into the Canadian Labour Congress in 1956.

p. 320 Joshua Tree: a national park east of Los Angeles, California, near Palm Springs.

p. 323 Dr Susumu Ohno: a Japanese-American geneticist and evolutionary biologist.

p. 327 Sharon Tate: an American actress, murdered in 1968 by the Manson Family when she was eight months pregnant.

Billy Curmano: an American performance artist.

Lewis St Louis: an American self-described as an "Artist-Designer-Visionary."

p. 335 "For a Sister": written in Windsor, early 1970s; published in *Up from the Kitchen, Up from the Bedroom, Up from Under: Women Unite!* (Canadian Women's Educational Press, 1972), 138. Never published in a collection by Wallace.

p. 336 “Labour Hearing”: unpublished typescript, dated October–November 1972. This and all the typescripts are in the editor’s possession.

Mike L: friend from Windsor, Ontario

p. 338 “The Baby Shower”: unpublished typescript, dated March 1976.

p. 341 “Sentimental Poem for My Mother”: published in *The Lance* (University of Windsor newspaper), 8 October 1976, 7.

p. 342 “You’ve Come a Long Way, Baby”: unpublished typescript, late 1970s.

p. 344 “Departures”: unpublished typescript, written in Kingston, early 1980s.

p. 346 “Like the Petit Point”: unpublished typescript, early 1980s.

p. 348 “We All Have Dreams”: unpublished typescript, early 1980s.

p. 350 “These Things Happen”: unpublished typescript, early 1980s.

p. 352 “They Say There’s Always a Worst,” unpublished typescript, mid-1980s.

p. 354 “Like All of Our Friends,” unpublished typescript, written in Kingston, early 1980s.

The third and fourth stanzas of “Like All of Our Friends” quote directly from, and refer directly to, the Matthew Arnold poem “Dover Beach.”

Bibliography

WORKS BY BRONWEN WALLACE

The Exploitation of Experience: Some Thoughts on the Study of Literature. Toronto: Hogtown Press, 1971. Pamphlet.

"Women's Lives: Alice Munro." In *The Human Elements: Critical Essays*, edited by David Helwig, 52–67. Ottawa: Oberon, 1978.

Marrying into the Family. Ottawa: Oberon, 1980. Poetry.

Signs of the Former Tenant. Ottawa: Oberon, 1983. Poetry.

Common Magic. Ottawa: Oberon, 1985. Poetry.

The Stubborn Particulars of Grace. Toronto: McClelland & Stewart, 1987. Poetry.

"In Other Words." *Kingston Whig-Standard*. Kingston, Ontario, 1987–88. Newspaper column.

Helwig, Maggie, and Bronwen Wallace, eds. *Coming Attractions 89*. Ottawa: Oberon, 1989. Edited anthology.

People You'd Trust Your Life To. Toronto: McClelland & Stewart, 1990. Short stories.

Keep That Candle Burning Bright and Other Poems. Toronto: Coach House Books, 1991. Poetry.

Arguments with the World: Essays by Bronwen Wallace. Edited by Joanne Page. Kingston: Quarry, 1992. Essays.

Mouré, Erin, and Bronwen Wallace. *Two Women Talking: Correspondence 1985–1987*. Edited by Susan McMaster. Toronto: Living Archives of the Feminist Caucus of the League of Canadian Poets, 1993. Letters.

Si c'est ça l'amour et autres nouvelles. Translated from the English by René-Daniel Dubois. Montreal: Les Allusifs, 2017. Short stories (French translation).

FILMS BY BRONWEN WALLACE

All You Have to Do, co-directed by Bronwen Wallace and Chris Whynot, 1982.

That's Why I'm Talking, co-directed by Bronwen Wallace and Chris Whynot, 1984.

WORKS ABOUT BRONWEN WALLACE

Atwood, Margaret. "Common Magic." Review of *Common Magic*, by Bronwen Wallace. *Journal of Canadian Poetry* 2 (1987): 120–3.

Barclay, Adèle. "Commemorating Common Magic." *The Queen's Journal*, 7 March 2008.

Bennett, Donna. "Bronwen Wallace and the Meditative Poem." *Queen's Quarterly* 98, no. 1 (spring 1991): 58–79.

Berry, Julie. "For Your 'Fine, Accurate Arms' – A Testimony to Bronwen Wallace." Brick Books website, 24 December 2015. https://www.brickbooks.ca/week-50-bronwen-wallace-presented-by-julie-berry/.

Black, Laura Carolyn. "'This Isn't One to Be Told in the Third Person': Social Activism in the Poetry and Prose Writing on Bronwen Wallace." MA thesis, Trent University, 1999. ProQuest.

Boire, Gary A. "Arbitrary Magic." Review of *Common Magic*, by Bronwen Wallace. *Canadian Literature* 110 (autumn 1986): 130–2.

Di Michele, Mary. "Author's Large-Spirited Feminism Will Be Missed." *Montreal Gazette*, 29 August 1992.

– "Bronwen Wallace: A Woman You'd Trust Your Life To." Review of *People You'd Trust Your Life To*, by Bronwen Wallace. *Montreal Gazette*, 14 April 1990.

Di Michele, Mary, and Barbara Godard. "'Patterns of Their Own Particular Ceremonies': A Conversation in an Elegiac Mode, between Mary Di Michele and Barbara Godard." In "Particular Arguments: A Special Issue on Bronwen Wallace," guest-edited by Susan Rudy Dorscht and Eric Savoy. *Open Letter* 7, no. 9 (winter 1991): 36–59.

Dorscht, Susan Rudy. "Writing at the Interval." In "Particular Arguments: A Special Issue on Bronwen Wallace," guest-edited by Susan Rudy Dorscht and Eric Savoy. *Open Letter* 7, no. 9 (winter 1991): 100–11.

Downie, Glen. "Forms for Argument." Review of *Arguments with the World*, by Bronwen Wallace. *Event* 22 (1993), 143–7.

Freiwald, Bina. "'This Isn't One to Be Told / in the Third Person': Wallace's Life Stories." In "Particular Arguments: A Special Issue on Bronwen Wallace," guest-edited by Susan Rudy Dorscht and Eric Savoy. *Open Letter* 7, no. 9 (winter 1991): 112–33.

Hatch, Ronald B. "Poetry." Review of *Common Magic*, by Bronwen Wallace. *University of Toronto Quarterly* 56, no. 1 (fall 1986): 35.

Hurlock, Debbie Ann. "Cadences of Voice, Conversations of Change: The Poetry of Bronwen Wallace." MA thesis, Lakehead University, 1996.

Keefer, Janice Kulyk. "Discoveries and Mysteries." Review of *Keep That Candle Burning Bright and Other Poems*, by Bronwen Wallace. *Canadian Literature* 138–9 (autumn/winter 1993): 131–3.

Kertzer, J.M. "'The Stubborn Arguments of the Particular.'" In "Particular Arguments: A Special Issue on Bronwen Wallace," guest-edited by Susan Rudy Dorscht and Eric Savoy. *Open Letter* 7, no. 9 (winter 1991): 71–87.

Laurin, Danielle. "L'amour entre détresse et enchantement: Bronwen Wallace et Brina Svit touchent avec finesse toute la complexité d'un sentiment." *Le Devoir*, 16 April 2017.

Lee, Dennis. "Bronwen Wallace's Work Crackled with Energy." *Globe and Mail*, 26 August 1989.

– "A Geography of Stories." In "Particular Arguments: A Special Issue on Bronwen Wallace," guest-edited by Susan Rudy Dorscht and Eric Savoy. *Open Letter* 7, no. 9 (winter 1991): 11–14.

Lynes, Jeanette. "Close-Ups." Review of *The Stubborn Particulars of Grace*, by Bronwen Wallace. *Canadian Literature* 122–3 (autumn/winter 1989): 212–15.

Manley-Tannis, Shelly Lynn. "'Dirt-Stained Fingernails': Bronwen Wallace Locating Her Self." MA thesis, Trent University, 1995. ProQuest.

Martin, Shelley. "Feminism, Motherhood, and Possibilities in the Writing of Bronwen Wallace." In *Feminist Mothering*, edited by Andrea O'Reilly, 61–72. Albany: State University of New York Press, 2008.

"The 'Morningside' Interviews." Transcribed and edited by Eric Savoy. In "Particular Arguments: A Special Issue on Bronwen Wallace," guest-edited by Susan Rudy Dorscht and Eric Savoy. *Open Letter* 7, no. 9 (winter 1991).

Mouré, Erin. "Ordinary Cranium." In "Particular Arguments: A Special Issue on Bronwen Wallace," guest-edited by Susan Rudy Dorscht and Eric Savoy. *Open Letter* 7, no. 9 (winter 1991).

Nixon-John, Gloria. "Getting the Word Out: The Country of Bronwen Wallace and Emmylou Harris." In *The Women of Country Music: A Reader*, edited by James E. Akenson and Charles K. Wolfe, 46–60. Lexington: University Press of Kentucky, 2003. Ebook.

– "A Place of Rupture: The Life and Poetry of Bronwen Wallace." PhD dissertation, Michigan State University, 2001. ProQuest.

Page, Joanne. "Bronwen Wallace: Legacy and Challenge." *The Kingston Whig-Standard,* 18 September 1989.

"RBC Bronwen Wallace Award for Emerging Writers." *Writers' Trust of Canada*. 21 May 2019. https://www.writerstrust.com/awards/rbc-bronwen-wallace-award-for-emerging-writers/.

Savoy, Eric. "The Antecedents of 'It': A Poetics of Absence." In "Particular Arguments: A Special Issue on Bronwen Wallace," guest-edited by Susan Rudy Dorscht and Eric Savoy. *Open Letter* 7, no. 9 (winter 1991): 88–99.

Schachter, Harvey. "Bronwen Wallace Tribute." *The Kingston Whig-Standard*, 31 August 1989.

Schaub, Danielle. "'A Landmark in Familiar Country': Alcohol in Bronwen Wallace's *People You'd Trust Your Life To*." *Études canadiennes/Canadian Studies: Revue interdisciplinaire des études canadiennes en France* 35 (1993): 231–44.

Scobie, Stephen. "The Voices of Elegy: or, Hurtin' Songs for Bronwen Wallace." *Bolder Flights: Essays on the Canadian Long Poem*, edited by Frank Tierney and Angela Arnold Robbeson, 151–9. Ottawa: University of Ottawa Press, 1999. Ebook.

Smart, Carolyn. "A Place at the Table." *Journal of Canadian Poetry* 5 (1990): 1–2.

Sniderman, W. "Feminist Nostalgia for Healing and Strength: Mnemonic Sites and Signs in Bronwen Wallace's Poetry and Prose." MA thesis, Memorial University of Newfoundland, 1996. ProQuest.

Vandenbeukel, Fay. "Interview with Bronwen Wallace." *Room of One's Own* 14, no. 1 (1991): 53–63.

Van Herk, Aritha. "Ghost Narratives: A Haunting." In "Particular Arguments: A Special Issue on Bronwen Wallace," guest-edited by Susan Rudy Dorscht and Eric Savoy. *Open Letter* 7, no. 9 (winter 1991): 61–70.

Vellino, Brenda C. "'A Network of Relations': Ethical Interdependence in Bronwen Wallace's Talking Lyric." In *Postmodernism and the Ethical Subject*, edited by Barbara Gabriel and Suzan Ilcan, 302–32. Montreal: McGill-Queen's University Press, 2004.

Verduyn, Christl. Review of *Arguments with the World: Essays by Bronwen Wallace*, edited by Joanne Page. *English Studies in Canada* 20, no. 1 (1994): 110–12.

Wainwright, J.A. "To Revelations." Review of *Marrying into the Family*, by Bronwen Wallace. *Canadian Literature* 91 (winter 1981): 148–51.

Webb, Phyllis. "Bronwen's Earrings." In "Particular Arguments: A Special Issue on Bronwen Wallace," guest-edited by Susan Rudy Dorscht and Eric Savoy. *Open Letter* 7, no. 9 (winter 1991).

Whalen, Terry. "Spiritual Autobiographies." Review of *Signs of the Former Tenant*, by Bronwen Wallace. *Canadian Literature* 103: 75–8.

Whitaker, Muriel. "Women Alone." Review of *People You'd Trust Your Life To*, by Bronwen Wallace. *Canadian Literature* 132 (spring 1992): 228–30.

Williamson, Janice. "Bronwen Wallace: '… I Couldn't Separate the Landscape from How I See My Poems Moving.'" In *Sounding Differences: Conversations with Seventeen Canadian Women Writers*, edited by Janice Williamson, 286–98. Toronto: University of Toronto Press, 1993.

– "'The Landscape from How I See My Poems Moving': An Interview with Bronwen Wallace." In "Particular Arguments: A Special Issue on Bronwen Wallace," guest-edited by Susan Rudy Dorscht and Eric Savoy. *Open Letter* 7, no. 9 (winter 1991).

Index of Titles